# Roadside With
## THE RMC RCL RMA RMF FRM

### Jim Blake

Route 477 was the last London Country trunk route, which connected Dartford and Orpington, to be operated by coach Routemasters - or any RM-types for that matter, lasting until January 1980. In typical late 1970s N.B.C. London Country condition, RMC1492 (SJ) heads towards Orpington along Crockenhill Road on 26th July 1978.

# Roadside With
# THE RMC RCL
# RMA
# RMF FRM

Published by Visions International Entertainment Limited

ISBN: 978-1-9126950-3-4

**Visions International Entertainment Limited**
**PO Box 12562, Chelmsford , Essex, CM3 3YA**
e-mail: deltic15@aol.com

For details of other bus and transport-related products, please visit the Visions web site:
http://www.visionsinternational.biz

# CONTENTS

# INTRODUCTION

**O**f the four prototype Routemasters which entered trial service between 1956 and 1958, one of them was a coach version, intended for busy Green Line cross-London services. This was originally numbered CRL4 (Coach Routemaster Leyland No.4): in common with the third Routemaster bus prototype, RML3, it had a Leyland engine and running units, and was unique in having Eastern Coachworks bodywork.

Equipped with platform doors, comfortable coach seats and luggage racks, it was tried out on various routes. Unlike other prototype double-deckers specifically built (or rebuilt) for Green Line use whose design was not perpetuated, it was judged to be a success, although some of its features bore a resemblance to those on RTC1, a wartime 2RT2 that had been substantially rebuilt as a prototype Green Line coach in 1949. Therefore, in 1961, London Transport placed an order with A.E.C. and Park Royal Vehicles for 68 coaches, classified RMC (Routemaster Coach, as which the prototype was also reclassified). Built in the late spring and summer of 1962, the first of these vehicles, which in most respects resembled the original, entered service on routes 715 and 715A at the end of August that year, with the rest following suit on other cross-London Green Line routes over the ensuing five months.

The new coaches, which seated 57 passengers, replaced the existing 39-seat RFs and were an instant success. However at this time too, a network of busy Green Line routes which radiated from Aldgate through the East End into south west Essex were operated by RTs. Apart from carrying Green Line livery and having saloon heaters (which by now were being fitted to many 'bus' RTs anyway), these RTs were no different to ordinary services buses. With the recent electrification of the London, Tilbury & Southend lines serving the same area as, and therefore competing with, Green Line, London Transport felt that these services should be improved. Thus in late 1964, another batch of coach Routemasters was ordered to replace the RTs operating Green Line routes based on Aldgate, into which anyway RMCs had already by then been operating on routes 720 and 720A. By now, production of 64-seat RMs was coming to and end, and they were going to be succeeded by the longer (30ft) 72-seat RML type. The second batch of Routemaster coaches were also of this length, and were classified RCL (Routemaster coach lengthened), seating 65 passengers. There were 43 in all, which entered service in the summer of 1965. Things did not quite go according to plan, since one of the 723 group of routes based at Grays (723B) was deemed to be difficult for the longer vehicles to negotiate, therefore RMCs were used instead and the spare RCLs exchanged with them on route 715A at Hertford.

Alas, the status quo with the new coaches did not last long. Ever increasing traffic congestion, particularly in Central London through which most of the RMC-operated routes passed, sabotaged the coaches' timekeeping. In the East, except at first on route 721 with which the new LT&S electric trains did not directly compete, the hoped-for revival of the Aldgate routes did not really materialise. Well before the loss of Green Line services to the new London Country entity, many of the RCLs had found their way to routes 704 and 705, crossing London from Windsor to Sevenoaks and Tunbridge Wells and the RMCs had also broken new ground; in one case - the 708 - to operate the route for only a year before being moved on elsewhere.

Meanwhile, a third type of coach Routemaster made its appearance in the winter of 1966/67 for British European Airways, for whom London Transport garaged, maintained and operated a fleet of 65 A.E.C. Regal IV coaches for their express service between Earls Court and Heathrow Airport. By the mid-1960s, these coaches (whose chassis were the same as RFs) were due for replacement and so 65 new Routemasters were ordered to replace them. These were short-length versions (the last such to be produced) and followed the general pattern of an A.E.C. Regent V (also with Park Royal bodywork) B.E.A. had

bought in 1962 and LT's own RMF1254 which they also used in the mid-1960s, by having forward entrances. They were otherwise given the same internal design as RMCs and RCLs, even down to the seat moquette, but were unique in that they towed a baggage trailer.

As will be explained more fully in the ensuing pages, within just two years of being taken over by London Country at the start of 1970, Green Line Routemasters began to be replaced by one-man operated single-deckers in the interests of economy. Those at Romford and Grays were the first victims, and indeed, at the latter garage, some RMCs had already begun to be used as ordinary Country Area buses even when they were still operated by London Transport. Following such predecessors as Qs, Ts, RTs and RFs, by the summer of 1972, all but a handful of Green Line Routemasters had been demoted to Country bus duties - at first in many cases being used on busy trunk routes such as the 370, 405 and 414.

The mid-1970s saw a number of London Country Routemasters (including RMLs too) falling victim to the nationwide spare parts shortage. The coach versions were relatively lucky in that only two RMCs and two RCLs succumbed to this, though many were off the road for a considerable time by the end of the decade having anyway been replaced by O.P.O. vehicles on bus duties too. But this was not the end for them. London Transport also were beset by problems with spare parts, made worse by the abysmal failure of their O.P.O. types - by this time, the awful DMSs especially. Indeed, as early as the autumn of 1975, a batch of thirteen 'B.E.A.' coaches (which had in fact by then passed to British Airways) had been acquired by London Transport and pressed into service on route 175 at Romford, releasing much-needed RTs for use elsewhere. It was just a matter of time before London Country Routemasters followed suit.

So, from the end of 1977 onwards, London Country RMCs and RCLs (as well as RMLs) began to be bought back by London Transport. At first, most were pressed into use - the coaches still in green livery - as driver training vehicles, releasing RTs back to service, even before the last Routemasters had been withdrawn by London Country, as they were on routes 407 and 477 early in 1980. By this time, most ex-Country RMLs had been overhauled in red and integrated with the rest of the fleet in front-line London service. In the latter part of 1980, the former coaches of the RCL class, many of which had been used as trainers after reacquisition by LT, were also overhauled as red buses and used to replace the hated DMs on route 149 in north London. Meanwhile, all of the Airways Routemaster coaches (whose Heathrow express service was finally withdrawn at the end of March 1979) had also been acquired by London Transport (who classified them RMA), and most of them initially found use as staff buses and driver trainers by the early 1980s.

Even that was not the end, since in later years Routemaster coaches of all three types found use with London Transport and its successors as sightseeing coaches, express buses and even ordinary service buses in London, as will be revealed in the ensuing pages of this book.

In addition, I have included the RMF, FRM and ERM varieties of the Routemaster herein, so that the three 'Roadside' books I have compiled include all types of this classic vehicle that have operated in the London area.

All of the photographs in this volume are my own; many having not been published before. I would like once again to thank the P.S.V. Circle and the London Omnibus Traction Society from whose records my own were derived in the earlier years, and also the website 'Ian's Bus Stop' for certain things of which I needed to be reminded all these years later. Thanks also go, as usual, to Colin Clarke who scanned all of my negatives a few years back as well as to Ken Carr, publisher of this series.

**Jim Blake**
**Palmers Green**
**November 2018**

---

*Main Cover Photo:* On 26th July 1978, RMC1492 (SJ) stands at Orpington, Goddington Lane, where it has terminated on a short journey from Orpington Station. Curiously, this was entirely within Greater London and therefore the former Central Area.

*Bottom Left Cover Photo:* British Airways Routemaster coaches were a familiar sight in Chiswick High Road during the 1970s, running to and from their depot and either Heathrow Airport or Earls Court in or out of service. BA55 is one of two heading for Heathrow at Turnham Green on 14th July 1978.

*Bottom Right Cover Photo:* Several RCLs retained Lincoln green livery, in which they had been overhauled in 1971/72 until the end of their London Country careers. On 23rd August 1978, RCL2250 (CM) heads for its home garage in Limpsfield Road, Sanderstead. Unlike those pictured later in this book working from Grays, however, somewhere along the line it has acquired a yellow waistband. Also of note is the upper-case lettering on its via blind, something several L.C.B.S. buses had at this time. Having come to Chelsham from Grays, it returned there upon route 403's OPO conversion two months after this picture was taken, being one of the last of all in L.C.B.S. service in January 1979.

*Back Cover Photo:* At Manor House on 16th October 1981, RCL2220 (EM) working route 279 passes RMC1502 which takes a break from training duties in a view that shows how the rear-ends of the two classes were identical.

# EARLY YEARS

On the first day of service of the production RMCs, Wednesday 29th August 1962, gleaming new RMC1463 (GF) calls at Manor House Station on its way from Hertford to Guildford on route 715. It is noteworthy how it appears to be carrying a full load of passengers. An RM on route 269 brings up the rear, whilst in front of the RMC, a British Railways van delivers publicity to a newsagents-cum-travel agent.

In addition to the commuter routes 721, 722, 723 and 723A, RCLs worked the summer limited stop route 726 to Whipsnade Zoo. On 12th July 1966, RCL2231 (RE) waits at the traffic lights in Aldgate High Street. Few, if any, passengers seem to be taking advantage of this luxurious form of transport from the East End to Bedfordshire! Of note is the altered livery from that originally used on RMCs, with the raised bullseye amidships replaced by a larger one (applied by stencil) nearer the front.

Also at Aldgate, RCL2253 (GY) awaits departure from Minories Bus & Coach Station for Tilbury Ferry on route 723A on 30th December 1966. Declining patronage of these routes meant the withdrawal of this service next day; the RCL's were redeployed to route 704.

By Good Friday, 24th March 1967, prototype RMC4 (HF)'s frontal appearance had been altered to resemble the production vehicles, except for retaining its non-opening front upper-deck windows. It still has light green piping around the windows, but bears the new bullseye symbol, as originally used on the RCLs. It has terminated at Victoria, Buckingham Palace Road on a short working of route 717.

After some five years in service, the production RMCs received their first overhauls at Aldenham Works. They had their own 'Works Float' to expedite the process, thereby changing bodies. On 9th November 1967, RMC1514 is about to be taken into Aldenham's famous oven for varnishing. As may be observed, the livery was altered at this stage, omitting the light green lining around the windows and the raised bullseye amidships. The larger RCL-style bullseye, applied by transfer, nearer the front of the vehicle was used instead.

Ten days later, on 19th November 1967, RMC1515 (SV) is still in original condition (apart from its front grilles) as it calls at Golders Green Station on its way from Hitchin to Chertsey on route 716, which along with the 716A, had been the last recipient of new RMCs in early 1963.

Nicely illustrating the new livery applied to RMCs upon their first overhauls, RMC1501 (SV) has just called at Hammersmith, Butterwick when working route 716A on 25th November 1967. Not many passengers are aboard on this somewhat bleak, cold Saturday.

On the same day as the previous picture, RCL2239 (TW) approaches Hammersmith (Met) Station on its way from Windsor to Tunbridge Wells on route 704. It too seems quite empty A few days later, the small Tunbridge Wells Garage, which only operated a handful of Green Line vehicles on this route, and not any other services, was closed and its allocation transferred to Dunton Green.

Newly-overhauled RMC1506 (HF) calls at Elephant & Castle Southern Region Station on Sunday, 26th November 1967 on route 717, shortly before this was withdrawn north of Baker Street and reverted to RF operation. It too has few passengers aboard, though the two old ladies at the coach stop on the right appear to be eager to board it.

Something of an oddity by late 1967 was Green Line route 709, which ran only on Monday to Friday rush hours, and on Sundays, between Baker Street Station and Godstone. It was allocated three RCLs, one of which, RCL2237 (GD), heads along North End, Croydon also on 26th November 1967.

Still in use on the first route to receive RCLs, the 721, RCL2219 (RE) stands at Aldgate, Minories on 3rd December 1967. Another detail difference between RMCs and RCLs was that the latter had wider front blindboxes, as may be appreciated by comparing the RCL with the RMC standing on the left.

At the end of November 1967, the experimental (and ultimately unsuccessful) RC class A.E.C. Reliance Green Line coaches on route 705 were replaced by RCLs after just two years' service. A month later, on 29th December 1967, RCL2260 (WR) crosses the junction of Lambeth Road and Kennington Road, near the Imperial War Museum. Once again, few passengers are in evidence although this is a lunchtime shot, not in the rush hour.

# AIRPORT EXPRESS - THE EARLY YEARS

On 17th December 1966, KGJ606D (BEA6), one of the first few forward-entrance Routemaster coaches operated by London Transport for British European Airways to enter service, accompanies 4RF4 MLL733 at the West London (Cromwell Curve) Air Terminal near Earls Court. As may be seen, these coaches had the same twin headlight arrangement as the RMCs and RCLs but did not have blindboxes. They also had fixed front windscreens.

At West London Air Terminal on 30th September 1967, a group of B.E.A. Routemaster coaches accompany Park Royal-bodied A.E.C. Regal IV MLL740, which for some reason was retained for a couple of years after its fellows. Clearly visible on the Routemasters is an offside illuminated panel between decks bearing the B.E.A. logo, similar to that borne on the nearside as illustrated below. NMY661E, of the second, 1967, batch is nearest the camera.

On 8th June 1969, B.E.A. Routemaster coach KGJ601D (BEA1, numerically the first of this type to be delivered) lays over at Heathrow Airport, complete with its luggage trailer. Of note is the panel above its entrance, which was illuminated.

At this period, the B.E.A. Routemaster coaches were undergoing a more drastic livery change than the RMCs and RCLs. A brash new livery of orange and white was replacing their original colours: NMY659E, one of the last to carry these, is outnumbered by those in the new style at Heathrow on 28th March 1970. The latter also lost their illuminated B.E.A. advertisement panels.

The B.E.A. Routemasters' maintenance by London Transport included heavy repairs and overhaul at Aldenham Works. On 4th October 1972, BEA23 (KGJ623D) arrives there on tow by A.E.C. Matador breakdown tender 750P. Some ten years later, this type of Routemaster would be seen every weekday at Aldenham, in very different circumstances, as will be revealed later in this book.

# LAST YEARS OF THE LT COUNTRY AREA

Into 1968, the penultimate year of London Transport's tenure of Country Area and Green Line services, and RMC1502 (GY) heads out of town along East India Dock Road, Poplar on route 723. By now, RMCs and RCLs were indiscriminately mixed on this route, and this one is of interest in that it has a wider front blindbox. This was done as a trial for the RCL class in 1964 on RMC1469, whose body passed to RMC1502 on overhaul in 1967.

On the same day as the previous picture was taken, RMC1503 (RE) bounces over the cobblestones at Stratford Broadway working route 721. This recently-overhauled RMC was, at this time, used as a float to cover RCLs going in for their first inter-overhaul repaints, explaining its unscheduled allocation to Romford, London Road Garage.

The RMCs displaced from the 717 when it was withdrawn north of Baker Street and reverted to RF operation late in 1967 went to replace RFs on route 708. At a snowy Eccleston Bridge, Victoria, RMC1510 (HH) heads for Hemel Hempstead on 9th January 1968, with few if any passengers aboard. RMC's would not last long on this route, as will be explained later in these pages.

By 18th February 1968, 'repaint float' RMC1503 (WR) has found its way onto route 704, covering for RCLs at Windsor Garage away for repaint. This view of it heading south towards Bromley Common was taken from the front upper-deck window of an RT travelling in the opposite direction.

A very well-filled RCL2226 (GD) on route 709 heads into Northumberland Avenue from Trafalgar Square in the evening rush hour of 29th March 1968, clearly showing the revised livery the RCLs were receiving upon intermediate repaint at this period. The principal change was the omission of their light green window surrounds, making them look somewhat blank without advertisements. The effect is made worse here by RCL2226 apparently having had its offside Green Line fleet name stencil scraped off! The RF behind the RMC is one of the former Green Line examples sold in 1964 to local operator Albert Harling, and used to transport nurses to and from hospitals in this area.

RMC1456 (WR) was also used at this period to cover for RCLs having their intermediate repaints. It calls at Slough town centre on route 705 on 1st June 1968.

On late summer Bank Holiday Monday, 2nd September 1968, RCL2224 (RE) has a good load aboard when calling at Golders Green Station on the way to Whipsnade Zoo. This was the last Bank Holiday the route ran, and it is interesting to wonder whether the passengers on it realised this.

On 6th February 1969, RMC1505 (EG) calls at Eccleston Bridge, Victoria on its way from East Grinstead to Hemel Hempstead. During the 1970s, this RMC would be one of two to fall victim to the vehicle spares shortage and, after being robbed of more parts to keep others of its class in service, was scrapped early in 1978. The other was RMC1509.

On a freezing 14th February 1969, RMC1516 (HH) awaits departure from Hemel Hempstead Bus Station for distant East Grinstead. Next day, route 708, which had only received RMCs in December 1967, would revert to RF operation amid savage service cuts to Green Line routes along the Brighton Road. These cuts resulted from loss of patronage.

Route 718 had been the second Green Line route to gain RMCs (in the autumn of 1962), working initially from Windsor and Epping Garages. When the latter closed in May 1963, they were reallocated to the new Harlow Garage which replaced it. RMC1479 (HA) is based there when passing through Camden Town on 2nd August 1969.

Few passengers are aboard RCL2228 (GY) as it passes the East Ham Odeon on its way to Aldgate on the 723 on Sunday, 12th October 1969. By now, the once busy Green Line routes terminating at that point were very much in decline.

On a wet and miserable 25th October 1969, RMC1515 (GY) approaches Grays War Memorial on one of the 723's short workings from Tilbury Ferry to East Ham. By now, some of these vehicles at Grays were being used to replace RTs on Country Area trunk route 370 from Tilbury to Romford.

Caught in the winter sunshine on 16th February 1970 as it is about to cross Lambeth Bridge on route 704 bound for Tunbridge Wells, RCL2240 (DG) is still to all outward appearances a London Transport vehicle, despite having passed to London Country at the beginning of the year.

Similarly to the RCL shown earlier on the 704, RMC1480 (HA) still carries its London Transport bullseyes both between decks and on its radiator badge when approaching Great Portland Street Station bound for Windsor some six weeks later, on 4th April 1970. However, its front via blind is somewhat odd, in that it does not show the usual 'Green Line' legend above the via points.

Four weeks later, on Saturday 2nd May 1970, a somewhat battered RMC1467 (HG) crosses the junction of Green Lanes and the North Circular Road at Palmers Green on route 715. Although it still carries LT bullseyes between decks, the one on its radiator badge has been painted out. A good number of passengers are on board, perhaps heading for Oxford Street or maybe the shopping centres at Wood Green, Holloway or Camden Town that this busy route also served.

*Right:* On a snowy 27th December 1970, my 23rd birthday, the driver of RCL2243 (GY) peers beneath its bonnet to make sure all is well before setting off for home from Aldgate, Minories Bus Station on the 723. By now, the RMCs and RCLs had shed their LT bullseyes and gained the London Country 'flying Polo' symbol on the panels behind their stairwells.

*Below:* Throughout 1971, the RCLs went to Aldenham Works for their first overhauls. RMCs were often used to cover for them, one of which, RMC1487 (GD) passes County Hall in the morning rush hour on 20th December 1971 on route 709, which within a few months of this picture being taken would be the only Green Line route still with a regular allocation of Routemaster coaches. Indeed, the three RCLs at Godstone for this route were three of the last to go in for overhaul, emerging in January 1972.

# LAST DAYS ON THE GREEN LINE

On 30th November 1971, RCL2221 (RE) rounds Gardiner's Corner, Aldgate - scene of the notorious Cable Street riots of 1936 - nearing the end of its journey from Brentwood, for which the driver has already set the destination blind for its return there. A month later, route 721, which had been the first Green Line to receive RCLs, would convert to RP O.M.O.

Well before their official demotion from Green Line coach to Country Bus status, a number of RMCs at Grays had been in use on various bus routes, notably the 370. On 27th December 1971 (yes, I was out photographing buses on my 24th birthday too!), RMC1475 (GY) sets off from Romford for Tilbury.

*Above:* Operation of coach Routemasters at Grays ceased at the end of 1971, too, with the 723 converted to RC O.M.O. and the 723A (a different version to that which ceased five years previously) withdrawn. On their final day, 31st December, RMC1471 (GY) awaits departure from Aldgate Minories Bus & Coach Station for Grays.

*Right:* With the RCLs being demoted to bus operation, the RMCs would soon follow suit. On 22nd January 1972, RMC1457 (GF) heads south along Tollington Road, Holloway on route 715A. This was a recently-introduced Saturday variation of the 715, which travelled via Kingston town centre rather than around the Kingston by-pass. The building on the right is Finsbury Park Diesel Depot, where, amongst other types, Deltics were housed at this period.

The RCLs on routes 704 and 705 were also replaced by new O.M.O. RPs in the spring of 1972. On 8th March that year, RCL2235 (DG) turns from Millbank onto Lambeth Bridge and is turning short at Dunton Green, perhaps owing to a staff cut, likely since conductors being made redundant shortly on this route were perhaps giving up the ghost early!

*Above:* On 4th March 1972, RMC1519 (WY) calls at Hyde Park Corner on its way to Woking on route 716A, a few days before O.M.O. RPs replaced RMCs on routes 716 and 716A. It is another to somewhat oddly show a front via blind without the 'Green Line' name.

*Below:* At the same time and place, but heading in the other direction, RMC1493 (WR) one of those allocated to Windsor for route 718, finds itself standing in for an RCL on route 704. However both routes will soon fall to the then all-conquering RPs!

*Above:* This lunchtime view on 21st March 1972 shows RCL2242 (DG) crossing Lambeth Bridge on sister route 705, bound for Windsor. Passengers used to the deep comfortable seats and spacious legroom on the RCLs were in for a rude shock when RPs with uncomfortable seats and cramped legroom replaced them!

*Right:* RMC1460 (HG) negotiates the Camden Town one-way system in Delancey Street alongside the West Coast Main Line on 22nd April 1972, the last day of RMC operation on the Saturday 715A.

Route 715 was the last Green Line service to have a full allocation of RMCs. In the evening rush hour of 24th April 1972, shortly before it too succumbed to the RPs, RMC1484 (GF) fills up with a long queue of commuters at Oxford Circus. Their numbers were swelled on this occasion by a strike on the Southern Region of British Rail if I recall correctly.

# LUXURY ON THE COUNTRY BUSES - RMCs AND RCLs DOWNGRADED!

On 3rd April 1972, recently-downgraded RMC1479 (DT) has turned short at Dartford Garage on route 401. Upon permanent downgrading to bus status, RMCs and RCLs received external advertising, which they never had as Green Line coaches, and this drastically altered their appearance. At Dartford, RMCs were more usually employed on routes 477 and 499.

Some months after demotion however, RMC1487 (HH) still has no external advertising, when heading through St. Albans in St. Peter's Street on 14th July 1972. Route 330 was a busy cross-country route linking Hemel Hempstead with Welwyn Garden City, on which RMCs were usefully employed to replace RTs.

Likewise, sister vehicle RMC1488 (SJ) is still advertless, though its fleetname has been altered from 'Green Line' to 'London Country', the latter being applied in yellow. It negotiates the roundabout at Orpington War Memorial near the end of its journey on route 477 from Dartford on 1st September 1972.

In the northern Country Area, the cross-country 341 also received RMCs in place of RTs. On 26th April 1973, RMC1509 (HF) stands at the old Hertford Bus Station working this route, which ran via Hatfield to St. Albans. This was the second of two RMCs to perish as a result of the vehicle spares shortage a few years later.

*Left:* RCLs as well as RMCs worked route 370 from Grays Garage following their demotion to bus status. On 2nd June 1973, RCL2246 (GY) has set down its last passengers at Romford Market Place before running around the corner to stand at Romford, London Road Garage. Of note is the fact that its front blindbox has for some reason been masked, thus obscuring the edges of its wider blind that should have fitted it!

*Centre:* Also based at Grays, RCL2241 (GY) has deposited its passengers at Epsom Downs racecourse on Derby Day, 6th June 1973, and sets off to collect another load from Epsom Station. In common with buses from all over the London Country system, it has been sent there for the day for the busy 406F. It was the only RCL at work on the route on this occasion, most other buses still being RTs, two of which are visible behind it.

*Below:* Some RMCs were also used on route 406F on Derby Day, 1973. In this view, RMC1478 (SJ) arrives at Epsom Downs with a full load of spectators. Also of note is the London Transport bus and coach 'dolly stop' on the right.

Trunk route 406, running from Kingston to Redhill and Reigate, ran right through the Epsom Downs racecourse, and by this time had received RMCs to replace its RTs - in theory at least, since the latter still worked it as late as January 1978! Also on 6th June 1973, RMC1459 (RG) is at Tattenham Corner and is turning short at Tolworth rather than going through to Kingston. The route still exists today as a London Buses service, running from Kingston to Epsom.

This was the era of all-over advertisement buses. London Transport's RMs and RMLs are best known, but a number of London Country vehicles - ANs and RPs - were also so treated along with a couple of RMCs. One was RMC1490 (RG) in a basically white livery promoting London and Manchester Assurance, and it speeds along Ashley Road, Epsom on its way to Kingston on the same day as the previous picture.

Important trunk routes 405 and 414 connected West Croydon with Horsham, and received RCLs in replacement of RTs early in 1972. Both ran to Redhill, from where the 405 continued via Crawley and the 414 via Dorking. On 28th December 1973, RCL2231 (DS) awaits departure from West Croydon Bus Station on a 'short' journey to Capel, which however is south of Dorking on the way to Horsham, so still a long way from Croydon! And is the inspector telling its driver that the RCL incorrectly shows a via blind for a local working in the Redhill area?

Sporting a battered dome that would increasingly become a feature of London Country Routemasters in their later years, RMC1485 (DT) climbs up East Hill out of Dartford town centre on 18th July 1974 on local route 499.

In 1974, British European Airways merged with the British Overseas Airways Corporation to become British Airways, and the 65 Airways Routemasters therefore transferred to the ownership of this entity. They were still maintained and operated by London Transport, and were going through their first overhaul cycle at the time. Although a new livery was adopted for them, some remained in the old B.E.A. orange and white livery, as borne by BA35 (NMY635E) which has just set down its passengers outside The Queen's Building, Heathrow on 28th August 1975. It was one of thirteen of them retaining this livery and just a couple of days later they were withdrawn: their subsequent fate is related later in these pages.

On the same day and at the same location, BA24 (KGJ624D) arrives at The Queen's Buidling, complete with luggage trailer. Its new British Airways livery of dark blue and white is already showing signs of wear and tear.

Much of the Airport Express Routemasters' journey to and from Heathrow was on the M4, therefore passengers had a very fast and comfortable ride. On 21st September 1975, BA19 (KGJ619D) is caught at speed on the M4 spur into Heathrow, and about to overtake a heavy lorry.

When new, the Airways Routemasters were housed at the former Chiswick Tram Depot, situated between Chiswick High Road and the District and Piccadilly Lines near Stamford Brook Station. Nearly ten years after the first was delivered, BA16 (KGJ616D) is one of three parked in its yard on 4th April 1976.

In the Chiswick and Hammersmith areas, Airways Routemasters could often be seen running dead to and from either the West London Air Terminal or Heathrow and Chiswick Tram Depot. On 4th March 1978, BA10 (KGJ610D) heads along Glenthorne Road, Hammermsith on its way to the W.L.A.T. It is minus its trailer, which will be attached at the terminal.

Following the opening of the Piccadilly Line's extension to Heathrow Airport in late 1977, the Airport Express service naturally lost passengers, and was therefore reduced. This meant that more of its Routemasters were redundant, and several were stored out of use at the West London Air Terminal. On 8th September 1978, BA20 and 16 (KGJ620D and KGJ616D) are clearly withdrawn, as also is BA13 (KGJ613D). However, by now it was virtually certain that London Transport would acquire them, as they already had others previously taken out of use by British Airways.

On the same day as the previous picture, BA6 (KGJ606D) and BA62 (NMY662E) stand in the rear yard of Stonebridge Park Garage, to where surviving members of the class had been transferred the previous month. Their garage at Chiswick was closed in order to be adapted for use a replacement for nearby Turnham Green Garage - it would reopen in May 1980, renamed Stamford Brook.

At the same location, BA12 (KGJ612D) stands inside the garage shed, accompanying an RML and an RT used on training duties. Behind the BA Routemaster may be seen some of the luggage trailers they towed. The wording of the advert on the front nearside of the vehicle is obviously meant to compete with the new Piccadilly Line extension to the airport, since having baggage in these coaches' trailers was more convenient than humping it in and out of the tube!

On 24th March 1979, BA37 stands in one of the loading bays at the Earl's Court West London Air Terminal. By now, not many people were using this express service to and from Heathrow, and it was withdrawn a week later. After all, as the adverts used to say, it was 'quicker by tube'!

Amply illustrating how the Airways Routemaster coaches operated with their luggage trailers, BA62 (NMY662E) speeds west bound for Heathrow on the Hammersmith Flyover on 30th March 1979, the day before this service ceased. It looks decidedly scruffy, and has few passengers aboard.

# RMCs AND RCLs TO THE RESCUE!

For many years, Country buses were used as Green Line reliefs to cope with extra passengers at busy times, particularly Bank Holiday weekends. Therefore it was no surprise that RMCs and RCLs originally used as Green Line coaches returned to their old haunts in this capacity after demotion. On Easter Monday, 3rd April 1972, RCL2219 (DG) is on route 705 at Eccleston Bridge, Victoria on loan from Reigate Garage and is about to run around the block to return to Sevenoaks. Its London Country fleetname and side adverts prove this to be after demotion, in fact only a few days after routes 704 and 705 lost their RCLs! A Country RML working relief on route 701 and a Green Line RF complete the picture.

Similarly, RMC1478 (SJ) heads across Elizabeth Bridge, Victoria on August Bank Holiday Monday 27th August 1973 working an extra on route 719 bound for the Brands Hatch race meeting that day. When new, RMCs had worked route 719 between Hemel Hempstead and Victoria, but were replaced by RFs when it was extended to Wrotham to replace route 717 late in 1968.

Also for a Brands Hatch race meeting, through for some reason showing the destination of nearby West Kingsdown, RMC1492 (SJ) heads south at Elephant & Castle B.R. Station on route 719 on 21st October 1973.

Towards the end of the RCLs' careers with London Country, when several had already returned to London Transport and were being used as driver trainers, RCL2251 (GY) has returned to its old haunts when departing from Aldgate Bus & Coach Station on 17th February 1978 for Grays on route 723. This is not a relief working in the sense that it is extra to the scheduled timetable - it is a desperation working, covering for failed O.P.O. vehicles! At this period, a handful of RCLs remained at Grays, usually used on school journeys. It is also noteworthy that it still retains its old Lincoln green livery, long after corporate N.B.C. light green had begun to replace this.

# THE N.B.C. LIVERY ERA

After a year or two carrying London Country Lincoln green livery, often with yellow waistbands and London Country fleetnames, RMCs and RCLs began to appear in corporate National Bus Company light green livery, in common with the company's RMLs. This was especially prevalent on the RMCs, which had their second Aldenham overhauls in 1974/75. On 15th April 1974, RMC1465 (SJ) has arrived at Eccleston Bridge, Victoria working a 719 Easter Monday relief from Brands Hatch.

On Derby Day 5th June 1974, newly-overhauled RMC1486 (RG) approaches Tattenham Corner amid Epsom Downs racecourse working back to its home garage on route 406. N.B.C. corporate green livery looked especially drab without external advertisements.

Also sporting the new N.B.C. livery, RMC1462 (DT) heads along Dartford High Street on local route 499 on 18th July 1974, as an RML on route 480 bound for Erith passes in the opposite direction.

*Above:* By the spring of 1975, the vehicle spares shortage was really becoming serious for London Country, and several of their RMLs were off the road as a result of it. In some cases, RMCs were drafted in to cover for them, as has happened on 19th April 1975 when Hemel Hempstead RMC1495 (GR) is on loan to Garston Garage working route 311 in Clarence Road, Watford.

*Left:* RMCs were based at Hemel Hempstead (Two Waters) Garage at this period replacing RTs on such routes as the 301, 302, 312, 320 and 378 - though they never did so completely. The 301 was the major trunk route through the area, running all the way from Bushey to Aylesbury. RMC1513 (HH) speeds through Berkhamstead on 22nd April 1975.

On the same day, RMC1498 (HH) loads up outside Hemel Hempstead Station in the evening rush hour, on local route 378 which ran between Apsley Mills and Gadebridge. It is noteworthy that the RMCs received the later RCL-style front wings upon their second overhauls, as clearly evident here.

During that evening too, RMC1491 (HH), apparently on loan from St. Albans Garage, climbs away from Two Waters on local route 312 heading for Hemel Hempstead new town. Some RFs and RTs in the yard of Two Waters Garage may just be glimpsed in the distance on the right behind the RMC.

Illustrating how London Country routes (and those of London Transport's Country Bus Department before them) frequently interworked, on the same evening RMC1498 (HH) which is shown above working to Gadebridge on route 378, is now heading away from Two Waters Garage for the same destination on route 320, unfortunately without showing via points. Such sloppy blind displays were by now becoming all too common on London Country vehicles.

*Above:* Also lacking via points on both front and side blind displays, RMC1513 (HH) heads past Bushey Hall Roundabout on 30th April 1975 on route 302. This route followed the 301 from Little Bushey to Two Waters Garage, where it diverged to continue to Hemel Hempstead New Town.

*Below:* At In the same area, RMC1455 (HH) has just been overhauled - one of the last to be done - and stands in for an RML on trunk route 347 (Hemel Hempstead to Uxbridge) when passing Bushey Arches on 10th July 1975. Its odd front blind display appears to be one from the side or rear of an RT, which type in any case was still also working route 347 at this time!

Fewer RCLs carried N.B.C. corporate livery, since all were overhauled in Lincoln green between February 1971 and January 1972, and did not receive another overhaul when in London Country ownership. Whereas several retained their original livery until the end, others had intermediate repaints in N.B.C. livery. One that did was the first of the batch; RCL2218 (DS), heads south along the Brighton Road through Purley on its long journey to Horsham on 11th September 1975.

As with the Epsom Derby and race meetings at Brands Hatch, extra buses were needed on route 410 for the annual Biggin Hill Air Show. On 20th September 1975, RMC1515 (GY) - one still with original RMC front wings - has come from Grays, and brings spectators back to Bromley along Oakley Road, Bromley Common.

# ENTER THE RMA's - AT ROMFORD!

A quite remarkable occurrence in the autumn of 1975 was the appearance of thirteen former British Airways (within which the former B.E.A. was now included) Routemaster coaches at Romford, North Street Garage in replacement of RTs on route 175. These had become surplus to B.A.'s requirements, and were snapped up by London Transport to help with the worsening vehicle spares shortages and pressed into service still in the former B.E.A. orange and white livery. Some of them still carried B.A. advertisements too, as does RMA11 (NS) heading for Chase Cross at the junction of North Street and the Eastern Avenue on 11th October 1975. As is obvious, these vehicles did not have blindboxes, therefore carried slipboards beneath their nearside canopies denoting which route they were on, as clearly shown here.

On the same day, RMA4 (NS) sets down passengers outside Central Park, Dagenham. It is turning short at Heathway, Pettits Road and has a slipboard specifically printed for this destination rather than the standard 'North Romford, Chase Cross and Dagenham New Road' display in the previous picture. Presumably, others existed for such short workings as to Romford Station, North Street Garage or Becontree Heath. The fact the RMAs were not fitted with blindboxes implies they were only intended as a short-term measure. Also, many passengers as first ignored them thinking they were 'workmens' buses' owing to their non-standard livery, whilst they were not popular with conductors due to not having the usual cubby-hole beneath the stairs for them to keep out of the way of passengers boarding and alighting.

At Dagenham New Road terminus on 10th January 1976, RMA2 (NS) is beginning to look quite shabby after three months' use on the 175. Of note is that the garage code and running number stencil-holders on these RMAs were removed from withdrawn MB-types, whose former garage codes they still displayed when first in service at Romford!

The RMAs' use on route 175 was not as short-lived as London Transport had hoped, therefore in the spring of 1976, they were repainted in standard red livery. Bizarrely, they were not done at Aldenham, but at their former home when in use as Airport Express coaches, the old Chiswick Tram Depot. This building had been used to overhaul and repaint non-standard bus and coach types (initially as an adjunct to nearby Chiswick Works) since its operational closure in the 1930s, and continued to do so when also in use to house the B.E.A./B.A. fleet. On 4th April 1976, RMA12 and RMA9 await a fresh coat of paint, which one of their fellows behind them has already received.

Smartly adorned in standard London Transport livery, complete with in-house advertisements, Airways Routemaster coach KGJ613D stands outside the old tram depot on the same occasion, with two of its fellows still in use for the airport service visible inside. It shows the fleetnumber RMA13, which logically it SHOULD carry. The problem is that this is not RMA13, but RMA38 - whereas the BEA fleetnumbers of these vehicles did accord with the last two digits of their registrations, their RMA numbers did not, since they were acquired haphazardly, as and when they became surplus to B.A. requirements and passed to London Transport, as all eventually did. This confused all and sundry, including myself, and still does today!

In its new red livery, RMA4 (NS) stands at the North Romford, Chase Cross terminus of route 175 on 9th April 1976. As may be seen, upon repaint, these RMAs were also given standard canopy number blinds, however it was alleged to be 'impossible' to fit them with full front blind displays. Subsequent events, as will appear later in these pages, proved this to be nonsense - clearly it was not deemed worthwhile bothering to fit them, and indeed the buses were withdrawn from service at the beginning of September 1976, although retained at first for non-passenger duties. It is also revealing that their repaints were only superficial, since the dents in RMA's dome match those it had when still in B.A. livery in the picture of it shown earlier!

# LAST OUTPOST IN THE EAST

By the latter half of the 1970s, it was just a matter of time before the RMCs and RCLs still in service were replaced by O.P.O. vehicles. One major surviving outpost of their operation was in the Grays and Tilbury area. Apart from the other major trunk routes detailed after this section, the important trunk route 370, linking Romford with Grays and Tilbury still used RMCs and RCLs. On 28th February 1976, RCL2251, still in Lincoln green, calls at a rather bleak-looking Feenan Highway in Tilbury.

On 1st April 1976, RCL2246 (GY), also still in Lincoln green, crosses the Mardyke River in Tank Hill Road, Purfleet on local route 374, which ran from Aveley to Linford, although it is turning short at Grays Garage.

Sister RCL2245 (GY), another in Lincoln green, heads along London Road, South Stifford on the same day on route 371. This route ran from Rainham to Tilbury, for which the destination 'Tilbury, Feenan Highway via Sandy Lane' is just squeezed into the blind!

*Above:* Another long-winded destination blind reading 'East Purfleet Mill Road via Stifford Clays' is borne by RMC1507 (GY) on route 375, also in London Road, South Stifford that day. This route served the industrial areas around Purfleet.

*Below:* Route 370A was another serving this industrial area. RMC1471 (GY), bound for Chadwell, Brentwood Road Estate, accompanies RCL2241 at the purpose-built bus terminus at East Purfleet, Thames Board Mills also on 1st April 1976.

At the same location, which was a nucleus for routes serving the industrial area here, sister RMC1472 (GY) has also arrived and works route 373, bound for Ockendon Station.

RMC1470 (GY) stands at Ockendon Station itself on a short working of local route 369 to Belhus, also on 1st April 1976. Many of these crew workings ceased shortly after I took these pictures, indeed RMC1470, 1471 and 1472 were all transferred to Chelsham to replace RTs on route 403 by the beginning of May.

*Left:* Working route 371 in Aveley High Street, RCL2221 (GY) stayed at Grays somewhat longer, until June 1977. It still clearly has a light green waistband, retaining the Green Line livery of 1967/68, apart of course from the LT bullseye and fleetname.

*Below:* Another route graced by Grays' RCLs which reached Rainham at this time was the 328: also on 1st April 1976, RCL2241 (GY) - another still in Green Line livery apart from the London Country fleetname and emblem - stands at Rainham War memorial terminus. What a contrast from the ugly red 'boxes' on the left!

RCL2241 (GY) has now received a repaint in corporate N.B.C. livery at some point, so still looks quite smart when passing along Corbets Tey Road, Upminster bound for Tilbury on 30th May 1977, immediately before route 370 converted to O.P.O. using BT class Bristol VRs with E.C.W. bodywork. In common with most of the RCLs displaced from Grays as a result, it was transferred to Chelsham to upgrade route 403, though returned to Grays in October.

Even after the 370 and most of the local services previously operated by RMCs and RCLs in Grays had converted to O.P.O., a few of the latter remained there. As shown by RCL2252 (GY) on 28th May 1978 in Grays town centre, these splendid vehicles suffered the ignominy of being used on school contracts at the end of their London Country careers!

At the very end, the RCLs at Grays did however still put in appearances on ordinary bus routes. On 15th September 1978, RCL2251 (GY), another still in Lincoln green, sets off from the garage for an evening rush hour stint on local route 323. Two Leyland Nationals inside the garage represent the type that saw most of them off.

*Left:* Somewhat oddly, Routemaster coaches remained on Green Line route 709 until the spring of 1976. Nominally RCL operated, it in fact had RMC1499 (GD) on loan to Godstone Garage at the very end. This heads for Baker Street around Park Crescent, Regent's Park on 2nd April 1976.

*Below:* On the 709's last day of crew operation, 14th May 1976, RCL2237 (GD) passes the Imperial War Museum on its way to Baker Street in the evening rush hour. This RCL was unique in that it was repainted in N.B.C. corporate livery, retaining its Green Line fleetname. It also has a large banner in its nearside lower-deck window proclaiming it to be the last official Green Line crew-operated double-decker to run.

On 21st May 1976, all-over advertisement RMC1490 (RG) passes South Croydon Garage on route 405, usually a preserve of RCLs at this period. Comparison with the picture of this RMC earlier in this book working route 406 will reveal this special livery is a different version to that carried previously.

Most of the last regular workings of London Country's RMCs and RCLs were on busy cross-country trunk routes, or those that radiated from the edge of Greater London out into the countryside. A good example was route 330, which ran from Hemel Hempstead to Welwyn Garden City via St. Albans, where on 16th October 1976, RMC1508 (SA) calls at the market place in St. Peter's Street.

Although busy trunk route 480 was one of the first, and also the last, to operate Country RMLs, RMCs were not usually to be found working it. However on 14th May 1977, RMC1457 (DT) does so, perhaps on loan to Northfleet Garage as it does not have a full blind display for the route. It heads along Queens Road, Erith near the start of its long journey to Gravesend.

Immediately after replacement on route 370 at Grays, the RCLs turned up on route 406F on Derby Day, 1st June 1977. A full RCL2238 (GY) calls at a splendid 1930s London Transport bus shelter in Ashley Road, Epsom and is about to be overtaken by a new Leyland National on the same route.

Just as the RCLs on route 370 were replaced by O.P.O. vehicles in the spring of 1977, so were those on routes 405 and 414 a few weeks later. On 28th June 1977, RCL2230 (DS) passes the quaintly-named Swan & Sugar Loaf pub in South End, Croydon bound for Capel on the latter route.

A little further south from the previous picture on the same day, RCL2258 (CY) heads along South End, Croydon on its way to Crawley. Route 405 still exists today running between West Croydon and Redhill as a London bus route.

Also on 28th June 1977 in South End, Croydon, RMC1501 (GD) finds itself working from Godstone Garage on route 409, usually the haunt of RMLs. It appears well filled and is also unusually terminating at Lingfield, instead of going through to East Grinstead and Forest Row.

Immediately prior to replacement by O.P.O. vehicles on route 330 and consequent withdrawal by London Country, RMC1498 (SA) passes Comet Corner, Hatfield on its way to Hemel Hempstead on 10th November 1977. By the end of that year, it will have been repurchased by London Transport, being one of the first RMCs to be employed by them as a trainer.

Routes 330 and 341 shared a common routeing for much of the way between St. Albans and Hatfield, both converting to O.P.O. in November 1977. On the same day as the previous picture, RMC1517 (HF) is at Smallford, passing a typical London Transport Country Area bus shelter and stop. This RMC moved on to Cheslham and then Grays, seeing almost two years' further use with London Country before it too returned to London Transport.

At Hatfield Garage itself on 10th November 1977, pioneer coach Routemaster RMC4 (HF) contrasts with one of the new Leyland Nationals that will replace RMCs on routes 330 and 341 next day, and has been working local route 840. This rear view emphasises a number of non-standard features on this prototype vehicle, not least the registration plate being on the offside, RT-style, rather than in the centre.

Route 477 was destined to be the last major London Country route operated by their former coach Routemasters, in this case RMCs. A major obstacle to converting it to O.P.O. was the three-point reversal turn necessary for school journeys terminating in the village of Crockenhill. On 26th July 1978, RMC1485 (SJ) has just performed this manoeuvre.

The busy 403, skirting the southern edge of Greater London and linking Wallington with Chelsham and Warlingham, was one of the last bastions of London Country RCL operation. On 17th August 1978, RCL2256 (CM) has terminated at West Croydon Bus Station from where it awaits departure to its home garage.

Several RCLs retained Lincoln green livery, in which they had been overhauled in 1971/72, until the end of their London Country careers. On 23rd August 1978, RCL2250 (CM) also heads for its home garage along Limpsfield Road, Sanderstead. Unlike those pictured earlier working from Grays, however, somewhere along the line it has acquired a yellow waistband. Also of note is the upper-case lettering on its via blind, something several L.C.B.S. buses had at this time. Having come to Chelsham from Grays, it returned there upon route 403's OPO conversion two months after this picture was taken, being one of the last of all in L.C.B.S. service in January 1979.

The smaller RMCs outlasted most RCLs at Chelsham Garage on route 403, due to the latter's certificates of fitness expiring during 1978, seven years after their last (and first!) overhauls. Also on 23rd August 1978, RMC1479 (CM) sets off for West Croydon from Warlingham Park Hospital.

The busy 406 also retained RMCs until their last years with London Country. On the same day as the previous picture was taken, RMC1475 (LH) crosses Epsom Downs bound for Kingston. All is quiet here on this occasion, in marked contrast to the scenes of this route on Derby Day earlier in this book!

As mentioned earlier, some of the very last RCLs in London Country service were at Grays, one of the three garages which had operated them when new in 1965. At the garage on 15th September 1978, RCL2247 (GY) has been at work on local route 328.

At this period, London Country was still suffering from the vehicle spares shortage, therefore a number of Routemasters were kept for emergency cover at various garages after their official allocations had ceaased, and used on virtually any route to cover for O.P.O. vehicles. On 21st September 1978, RMC1512 (HF) finds itself on local route G4 and is about to cross the Great Northern main line at Welwyn Garden City. Of note is the very improvised blind display!

RCL2259 (CM) is still in Lincoln Green livery as it gleams in the autumn sun at Reeves Corner, Croydon on 11th October 1978. At that time, few if anyone could have foreseen that twenty-two years later, trams would be running along this stretch of road, or that the famous Reeves department store would be destroyed by fire in the dreadful race riots of summer 2011. The RCL is one of the last in use at Chelsham, and upon the main service on the 403 converting to O.P.O. a few days after this picture was taken, would also return to Grays for another two months' service.

Somewhat curiously, route 403's Express journeys remained Routemaster operated for some months after its main service converted to O.P.O. On 3rd April 1979, RMC1511 (CM) sets off from West Croydon for Warlingham. This RMC would be one of the very last in London Country service.

Country Area route 493 ran locally in the Orpington area, most oddly entirely within Greater London. Also, strangely, it was one of the very last London Country routes to retain Routemasters, with its allocation derived from route 477 at Chelsham Garage. On 21st October 1979, RMC1512 (SJ) negotiates the turning circle at Orpington Station. This RMC would be last of all in use with London Country a few months later.

On New Year's Day, 1980, RMC1485 (SJ) stands at the Dartford, Joyce Green Hospital terminus of route 477, immediately before replacement by O.P.O. vehicles.

On 1st March 1980, London Country organised a farewell tour for their 'Routmasters' as the word is quaintly misspelled on the blind of RMC1512 (SJ), passing the Mark Inn at Keston. It was accompanied by RML2446 - both passed back to London Transport soon afterwards.

# AWAITING THEIR FATE

On 16th July 1977, RCL2227 makes a sad sight dumped in the yard of Grays Garage along with other defunct vehicles. It had expired at Reigate Garage in October 1974 at the height of the vehicle spares shortage crisis, and been gradually cannibalised to keep others in service. Sadly, it was one of two RCLs to go for scrap, along with two RMCs, at the end of 1977.

Odd RMCs and RCLs could be found out of action at many London Country garages at this time. Also looking sorry for itself, RMC1482 is stored outside Hatfield Garage, where it had been withdrawn in October 1977, on 13th September 1978. In the event, it would never run again despite being acquired by London Transport the following summer.

Both when replaced by O.P.O. vehicles and, in the case of the RCLs, when their certificates of fitness expired seven years after overhaul, London Country's Routemasters were often just left stored in the open outside their former garages in their last years. On 6th September 1978, RCL2246 is one of several languishing in the yard outside Chelsham Garage, and for some reason a red London Transport RT trainer accompanies them. By this time, London Country Routemasters of all three types were returning to London Transport.

It was not only London Country Routemasters which had an uncertain fate as the 1970s drew to a close, but also the British Airways ones. Their Earls Court to Heathrow service was finally withdrawn at the end of March 1979, and many of the vehicles that had remained in service until then went into store at Fulwell Garage. On 2nd April, these seven viewed from inside Fulwell are amongst a group stored in the rear yard flanking Stanley Road. In June, all were bought by London Transport meaning that all 65 vehicles were now in their ownership.

On 12th May 1979, RMC1487 and RMC1501 are out of use outside Chelsham Garage, despite still carrying 403 blinds. They flank a badly cannibalised RCL2243. This was one of many delicensed Routemasters robbed for spare parts to keep others going at this period, though in the event, it would run again.

By this time, London Country had so many defunct and withdrawn vehicles, mostly Routemasters, that they were obstructing service buses at many of their garages. Therefore, the company hired secure storage space at the disused Radlett Aerodrome to accommodate them. On 19th May 1979, three RMCs and an RCL await their fate there alongside the Midland main line. A few weeks later, all were bought by London Transport.

On 24th May 1979, RMC1460 languishes outside Swanley Garage, where it has been cannibalised to keep others in service there on routes 477 and 493 after expiring in April 1978. It too never ran again despite passing to London Transport a few weeks after this picture was taken.

Following purchase by London Transport, many former London Country Routemasters were stored, most ironically at the former A.E.C. Works at Southall, which had recently been closed. On 13th April 1980, RCL2228 and RCL2243 are nearest the camera in this long line of them. In the event, all of the RMLs and all but one RCL were overhauled for use as red buses, whereas the RMCs found use as trainers - though not all of them did so; most of those not used eventually went for scrap.

Not all of the Airways Routemasters were to be used by London Transport, either. Cannibalised RMA45 (KGJ625D) makes a sad sight dumped at the back of Stonebridge Park Depot on 10th May 1980. It would remain there until going for scrap more than a year later.

Still in Stonebridge Park Garage over a year later on 16th May 1981, RMA17 (ex-BEA17), RMA2 (ex-BEA26) and RMA43 (ex-BEA23) have also been heavily cannibalised before going for scrap. The two still in BA livery were also never used by LT, RMA2 in the middle had had a very short service life with LT - just eight months or so at Romford on route 175, and then ten months as a staff bus at Hounslow.

Also heavily cannibalised is RMC1479, which had been withdrawn from Chelsham Garage in February 1979, and stands outside Camberwell Garage with a group of withdrawn MBAs and DMSs on 20th July 1981. Along with them, it went for scrap soon afterwards, having in fact been sold officially to Wombwell Diesels before this picture was taken!

Numbered RMA49 but never used by London Transport, NMY632E was one of the lucky ones. With a group of others, it stands in the disused A.E.C. Southall Works on 1st September 1982 awaiting its fate. Shortly afterwards, it was acquired for preservation and subsequently passed to the Blue Triangle fleet, as will be shown later in this book.

# LEARNING THE GAME

From early February 1977, some of the RMAs that had been used on route 175 began to appear as driver trainers. Owing to the need to have the instructor seated behind the novice driver and equipped with emergency braking equipment, their forward staircases were removed and an extra offside lower deck window placed where the stairwell had been. This modification is clearly visible in this unusual view of RMA4 in Lordship Lane, Wood Green, taken from the side window of an RML heading in the other direction on 7th February 1977.

As 1977 progressed, it became increasingly obvious that the growing number of redundant London Country Routemasters would be reacquired by London Transport, though for what exact purpose was at first unclear. Then, in December of that year, examples of all three types began to be bought back by LT. The RMLs were, at first, either taken to Aldenham for overhaul or merely repainted red and pressed into service, whereas RMCs and RCLs were put on training duties, still in London Country livery. On 8th January 1978, RMC1516 is being checked over in Stonebridge Park Garage prior to taking up training duties.

RCL2254 was one of the first of its type to be employed by London Transport as a trainer after reacquisition. On 3rd February 1978, it arrives at Streatham Garage, having been given an LT roundel and in-house adverts on its N.B.C. light green livery. It also has new wings, still in pink primer, presumably after accidental damage.

The RMCs used by London Transport on training duties were similarly treated initially: RMC1497 is based at Brixton and turns out of King William Street at Monument Station on 17th Febraury 1978.

Another RMC reacquired by London Transport and assigned to training duties early in 1978 was RMC1507. Curiously, when in this role on 4th May 1978 in Ladbroke Grove, it lacks both a front 'private' blind and LT bullseyes. For no apparent reason, not long afterwards it was sold privately for preservation and is restored in original 1962 Green Line livery today.

After some months on training duties, the RMAs were given 'Private' blind displays pasted onto where their blindboxes would have been, presumably so as not to confuse intending passengers. At lunchtime on 3rd July 1978, RMA3 passes the imposing clocktower at Crouch End Broadway.

*Top:* Coming in the other direction almost immediately afterwards, RCL2233 is likewise employed on training duties that lunchtime. Of note is its side advertisement specifically aimed at recruiting drivers.

*Centre:* After a flurry of activity acquiring Country Routemasters at the end of 1977 and into 1978, their intake slowed to a trickle. This was apparently owing to LT insisting that they be received in serviceable condition, which was apparently difficult for L.C.B.S. who were struggling to keep their own vehicles on the road. To illustrate this, RCL2218 had been delivered to Clapham Garage (then in use as a store for new or withdrawn vehicles) in March 1978, but then after some months returned to London Country at Grays. It finally came back to LT in February 1979, and was placed in service as a trainer still bearing London Country fleetnames and adverts! On 11th March that year, it pulls off the stand at Tottenham Court Road Station into St. Giles High Street.

*Bottom:* In complete contrast, something of a stir was caused when RCL2232, a trainer that had been at Bow Garage throughout 1978, was painted in current red London Transport livery. It circumnavigates the roundabout at Fullwell Cross, Barkingside on a snowy 18th March 1979. I remember remarking to a friend who was with me at the time how nice they would look in that livery as red buses, not realising my words would come true in the summer of 1980, as will be revealed later in this book!

Since several RCLs ended their London Country careers still bearing Lincoln green livery, it was inevitable that some would reach London Transport in that condition, and be used as trainers still carrying it. Thus is RCL2250 so adorned when heading along Barkingside High Street on 7th April 1979, having recently been allocated to Wood Green Garage. It is of note than unlike the N.B.C. green-liveried examples, it does not have an LT bullseye.

At a time when green RMCs and RCLs were becoming a fairly common sight being used on training duties for London Transport still in London Country N.B.C. light green corporate livery, RMC1453 starts the steep climb up Highgate Hill from Archway Station on 22nd August 1979. It is however still with London Country, allocated to Hatfield Garage. The badly dented front dome is of note. It would later pass to London Transport and be used in the same role, but in red!

A much more minor change in livery is sported by RMC1459 approaching Hackney Station on 27th August 1969. It still carries N.B.C. light green livery, but has had its mudguards painted black, whereas hitherto they were also light green.

As the 1970s drew to a close, those former Country Routemasters in use as trainers began to get more and more shabby. The badly dented dome on RMC1489 parked outside Walworth Garage on 29th August 1979 illustrates this.

RCL2259 had been in use at Stonebridge Park Garage as a trainer since January 1979, still bearing Lincoln green livery and as this view shows also acquired bullseyes. However on 10th May 1980, it is out of action and will not be used in this role again - instead it will go to Aldenham for overhaul.

Inevitably, after some two and a half years working as trainers for London Transport, most of the RMC former coaches were repainted in standard red livery. The work was done at Aldenham Works, outside whose huge building RMC1475 stands on 18th September 1980. However, as is evident, in most cases, the dents on their roof domes were merely painted over rather than being infilled or replaced with new ones.

By the summer of 1981, several of the final batch of RMAs acquired by LT in 1979 were in use as driver trainers. Unlike those used as staff buses, all were painted red before assuming this role. Aside from some small dents in the front dome, RMA47 looks very smart outside the L.T. divisional offices at Manor House at lunchtime on 16th July 1981, its instructor and trainees having popped in for a cup of tea.

After a while these red-painted trainer RMAs of the third batch began to receive external advertisements and special 'blind' displays at the front. Also clearly showing how its staircase has been removed, RMA38 approaches Edmonton, Cambridge roundabout on 26th February 1982.

On 7th August 1982, RMC1453 - numerically the first production-batch RMC - is one of two standing in the former coal yard used as an overspill for buses based at Kingston Garage, and despite being repainted in red livery, still has the same dents in its front dome that it had nearly three years previously when training for London Country, as illustrated earlier!

Both RMAs and RMCs operated at the Chiswick Training School until its last days. On 9th May 1986, RMA40 sets off from there on a training mission. An RMC and one of the RMLs used to familiarise drivers with these longer vehicles stand to the left, on the right is the 'Chiswick Experimental' RM1368 which had been reduced to single-deck after an arson attack many years before, along with a DMS used as a trainer.

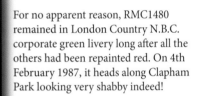

For no apparent reason, RMC1480 remained in London Country N.B.C. corporate green livery long after all the others had been repainted red. On 4th February 1987, it heads along Clapham Park looking very shabby indeed!

In their last years as driver trainers, RMCs in red livery too became quite shabby, as this unusual view of RMC1462 at Wandsworth Garage on 26th June 1987 shows. The garage was closed to normal service buses a couple of weeks later, but then used for the Original London Transport Sightseeing Tour fleet.

# LUXURY STAFF TRANSPORT!

The 65 British Airways Routemaster coaches were acquired by London Transport in three batches. The first thirteen, acquired at the end of August 1975, were used initially on route 175 at Romford, and then as either staff buses or trainers. Another fourteen were obtained in November 1976, and all but two of these became staff buses during 1978. On 21st September that year, RMA26 leaves Aldenham Works. It has had its British Airways branding removed, whereas the one following still carries this.

In contrast, RMA23, acquired at the same time, has been smartly painted in standard red livery. An SM follows - these contraptions were generally replaced by the RMAs which obviously gave staff a luxurious ride as well as a more breakdown-free one!

Also leaving Aldenham Works that day, RMA6, the former Romford North Street engineers' bus, has also been appropriated for staff bus duties. One of the last RTs in such use, which the RMAs also replaced, follows it on Elstree Hill.

Long after the split between the Central and Country Areas of London Transport, and the consequent formation of London Country, LT-owned staff buses were still based at former Country Area garages, taking staff from the relevant areas to and from Aldenham or Chiswick Works. Therefore, RMAs found their way to these garages and on 19th May 1979, RMA19 stands outside Garston Garage.

RMAs predominate in this line-up of staff buses awaiting their passengers at Aldenham Works on 2nd August 1979, with just one SM intruding. Most, if not all, are from the batch bought in 1976.

Leaving Aldenham on the same day, RMA63, still in British Airways livery, is one of the third and final batch of 38 RMAs acquired by London Transport in June 1979. Twenty-one of these had been put into use as staff buses by the end of the year, of which this one is one of few RMAs which by coincidence had a matching fleet and registration number. Of the remainder, others became both staff buses and trainers during 1980, though in the event some of them would never be used by London Transport.

Some RMAs used as staff buses were given in-house London Transport adverts while still in British Airways blue and white livery. On 15th May 1980, RMA46 heads along Burlington Road, Chiswick taking staff home to Abbey Wood from the nearby Works.

Also bearing LT in-house advertisements and the remnants of British Airways livery, Hackney staff bus RMA48 passes Finsbury Park Station on its way back from Chiswick Works on 11th August 1980. Its shabby external appearance belies its luxurious interior!

Despite bearing a Chiswick slipboard in its windscreen, RMA50 is in fact at Aldenham on 25th March 1982, awaiting the homegoing workers. By now it is one of few still in British Airways colours; also all staff buses on this occasion are RMAs.

*Top:* Looking somewhat sorry for itself and accompanying what appear to be two newly-overhauled engines and some London Transport service vehicles at Chiswick Works on 3rd July 1983, RMA1 is still in use as a staff bus. Its orange and white B.E.A. logo from 1969/70 has reappeared beneath its red paint at the front!

*Centre:* At the end of their careers as staff buses, the RMAs became quite shabby even in red livery. On 24th September 1986, only two months before Aldenham Works closed, an apparently empty RMA7, one of those that had been used on route 175, heads through Enfield Town on its way back to Leyton.

*Bottom:* A final livery borne by RMA staff buses in London was that of Bus Engineering Ltd, which the L.R.T. regime had privatised from the remnants of Chiswick Works at the beginning of 1985. On 18th March 1987, RMA8 is on its way taking workers from there home to St. Albans - thus RMAs were stationed in the former Country Area until the last! It would later be returned to service at Upton Park Garage. Meanwhile, B.E.L. withdrew their last RMA staff buses in December 1987.

**Roadside With THE RMC, RCL, RMA, RMF & FRM**

# RCL REPRIEVE

Although all of the RCL's, except for the two scrapped at the beginning of 1978, had been reacquired by London Transport by the autumn of 1979, by no means all of them were employed on training duties. Many had been off the road for a long time, usually in open storage and needed a lot of work done on them. A typical example was RCL2240, which had been out of use since September 1978. On 9th December 1979, it is in the rear yard of Bexleyheath Garage where it is apparently being examined - somewhat odd when this garage never had Routemasters operationally!

Since the awful crew-operated DMs were proving just as much a disaster in service as the O.P.O. DMSs, it was decided to overhaul the RCLs and return them to service to replace them. Work on them began in the summer of 1980, and to my glee, the route chosen for them to replace DMs on was the 149, running quite locally to me. On 9th August 1980, the day before the first entered service, sparkling newly-overhauled RCL2223 (SF) accompanies DM1731 in Stamford Hill Garage, already blinded up for its new route. A noteworthy change upon overhaul was the removal of the twin headlamps that had been common to all three coach Routemaster types, and their replacement by standard RM ones. In fact this RCL has the earlier type of RM headlamps and wings, with the brake cooling grilles filled in.

Another change to the RCLs upon overhaul was the removal of their platform doors and the provision of extra grab-rails on their platforms. However they retained their non-standard rear-ends, complete with emergency exit doors. RCL2257 (SF) illustrates this, also in Stamford Hill Garage on the day before they entered service. Internally, they retained their coach seats, thereby seating 65 passengers (only one more than an RM) but their luggage racks were removed. They still lacked stanchions, however, and this proved to be a cause of passenger complaints, especially from the many elderly people who relied on their local buses.

Early on the morning of Sunday 10th August 1980, RCL2249 (SF) runs out from its garage for the first time on the day these splendid vehicles re-entered service. Their introduction was gradual, starting at Stamford Hill, though most buses from that garage on the 149 were RCLs on the first day. This one has the later type of RM/RML wings, without brake cooling grilles.

Just around the corner, RCL2242 (SF) makes a splendid sight escorting a DM across the junction of Stamford Hill, Clapton Common and Amhurst Park. Recalling when they were new on Green Line service fifteen years before, they ran for some time at first without any external advertising, looking very splendid indeed. In fact, many passengers thought they were new, as of course their deep, comfortable coach seats were newly-trimmed in standard Routemaster moquette during their Aldenham overhauls. They were indeed a contrast to the uncomfortable, rattling box-like contraptions they replaced, one of which follows!

From the start of their use as red buses, I set about photographing every one of them, both front and especially rear, in case at some later stage they were overhauled again and rebuilt with standard RM backs. In the event, they were not to have another overhaul as such, but as will be explained later, it is fortunate that I took this rear shot of RCL2256 (SF) heading north along Kingsland Road, Dalston, also on the first day.

On Saturdays and Sundays at this period, route 149 ran only from Ponders End to Liverpool Street - the section beyond the latter point to Waterloo and Victoria working only on Mondays to Fridays. Buses had two different sets of via blinds for these workings; those from the south usually going only as far north as Stamford Hill. Returning from Liverpool Street beneath the bridge carrying the long closed North London Railway Shoreditch Station, closed during the war and then occupied by Alfred Goldberg's dressmaking business, RCL2242 (SF) correctly shows the via blind for the 149's northern section.

Monday, 11th August, the 149's first day of running through the City and full rush hour working, was a horrible wet one, but that did not deter me from photographing them! RCL2222 (SF) collects passengers in a soggy Stoke Newington High Street, correctly showing the via points for the 149's inner section to Victoria.

Just over a week later on 18th August 1980, an apparently empty RCL2218 (SF) gleams in the sun as it crosses Lambeth Bridge at lunchtime heading for Victoria. Such a sight would have been unthinkable between 1967 and 1972 when these vehicles could be seen at the same spot on Green Line routes 704 and 705!

After some five or six weeks, Stamford Hill's allocation of RCLs for the 149 was complete, and then a start was made on allocating them to Edmonton Garage to complete conversion of the route. Newly-overhauled RCL2253 (EM) awaits entry into service there on 20th September 1980.

Three weeks later, they entered service from Edmonton Garage. On 11th October 1980, an immaculate RCL2226 (EM) departs from Edmonton Green Bus Station for its home garage, with one of the dreadful tower blocks built above the adjacent shopping centre as a backdrop and an incorrect via blind for the route's southern section, which buses from this garage seldom reached!

By this time, the Stamford Hill RCLs had been in service for up to two months, and began to receive external advertising. On the same day as the previous picture, RCL2258 (SF) heads south along Fore Street, Upper Edmonton. It too displays the wrong via blind!

Back at Edmonton Green, still then referred to as Lower Edmonton Station, RCL2257 (SF) has turned short as RCL2223 (SF) - again with the wrong via blind - heads for Ponders End, also on 11th October 1980. In more recent times, the bus station here has been substantially enlarged and roofed, while the monstrous multi-storey car park behind the two 149s is no more.

With its home, Edmonton Garage, visible in the distance, RCL2241 (EM) has just been given a turn at Dalston, Downham Road rather than going through to Liverpool Street by the inspector in his box at the corner of Tramway Avenue and the Hertford Road on 23rd November 1980. By now, the allocation of RCLs to the 149 was almost complete.

Perhaps because it had been so badly cannibalised whilst in store with London Country, RCL2243 (SF) was the last to be overhauled as a red bus, not entering service until early 1981. It went to Stamford Hill rather than Edmonton, and on 14th February 1981 heads past the Passmore Edwards Library in Fore Street, Upper Edmonton once again displaying the wrong via blind for the 149's northern section of route!

# RCL ROGUE WORKINGS

Although the RCLs were intended to replace crew DMs on route 149 after their overhaul as red buses, they were regarded at both Stamford Hill and, later, Edmonton Garages as being the same as their RMs, and therefore used on all crew routes at each garage as well. On only their second day in service, 11th August 1980, RCL2246 (SF) has turned short at Dalston, Downham Road on normally RML-operated route 243. DMs were never used on this route.

Next day, 12th August 1980, RCL2240 (SF) is also working the 243, and loads up in the morning rush hour at the route's first stop in Lordship Lane, Wood Green, opposite the Eastern National depot that had gained fame some years earlier when the 'On The Buses' TV series was filmed there. As may be observed, the partly enclosed platform on the RCLs impeded loading somewhat and therefore slowed the buses up (though not as much as the twin-door DMs they replaced!) and could explain why the RCL has been curtailed at Old Street Station.

The RCLs soon made their presence felt on the busy 253, on which Stamford Hill had a part allocation. No doubt these smart vehicles, epitomised by RCL2249 (SF) passing beneath the North London Line at Camden Road Station on 19th August 1980, put the scruffy RMs fielded by Holloway Garage on this route to shame!

The RCLs also found their way onto Sunday-only route 243A; in fact on 24th August 1980, a fortnight after their introduction, two of them were at work on it. One was RCL2240, the other, RCL2246 (SF), has turned short at Tottenham, Bruce Grove Station and stands at the Woodside Gardens terminus that was the northern end of route 171 for many years.

It was even possible to catch two RCLs together on unscheduled workings, as at Stamford Hill Broadway on 12th September 1980, when RCL2250 (SF) overtakes RCL2255 (SF) having a crew change on route 243!

Inevitably, the RCLs at Edmonton soon found their way onto route 279, which had recently been re-extended to Hammond Street when graced by RCL2231 (EM) on 16th November 1980. It escorts another RCL along Fore Street approaching its junction with the North Circular Road. The 279 too usually ran in two overlapping sections and had two different via blind displays: this one is incorrect for the outer section of the route.

A far cry from its condition when languishing in the field behind Chelsham Garage for best part of eighteen months, sparkling RCL2220 (EM) calls at Manor House on 18th November 1980 on the 'inner' section of the 279, which nevertheless ran all the way from Smithfield on the edge of the City of London to Waltham Cross, just over the Greater London border into Hertfordshire.

On 30th November 1980, RCL2231 (EM) gleams in the winter sunshine as it passes Edmonton Police Station in Fore Street, with stablemate RCL2230 in pursuit. It is working the Sunday 279A, and unusually turning short at Tottenham Garage.

A week later, on 7th December 1980, RCL2252 (EM) is also working the Sunday 279A and has terminated at Hammond Street, one of the northernmost points that London Transport Central Area buses ever reached. Of note is that it has a different number and via blind to the RCL in the previous picture, as the 279A also ran in two overlapping sections.

*Above:* Recently-overhauled or not, RCL2244 (EM) has come to grief working route 279 on 13th December 1980 when approaching Lower Edmonton Station, and needs to have its offside front wheel changed. Fitters have come out to it in D 923, one of the vehicles the RCLs have displaced which however for the time being is retained as a spare, and adapted to work either as a crew or OPO bus. They have upheld the time-honoured tradition of placing one of the RCL's seats against its back to indicate it is immobile.

*Left:* On 21st December 1980, RCL2226 (EM) is well-filled with shoppers from Chapel Market as it passes Islington Town Hall on its way to its home garage on the Sunday 279A.

Two Edmonton RCLs, RCL2226 and 2245 (EM), have arrived at the Smithfield terminus of route 279 together on 28th July 1981 as a third bus on the route, one of its scheduled standard RMs arrives there.

# AT ALDENHAM

On 26th May 1977, British Airways coach NMY662E has had extensive frontal repairs done to it at Aldenham, evidenced by the new paintwork between decks and on its bonnet and wings. Little did I know when I took this photograph that within a few months, Routemasters in B.A. colours would be a familiar sight there working as staff buses - including this one!

At the time the RCLs were beginning to enter service as red buses in the summer and autumn of 1980, examples of all three varieties of Routemaster coaches were receiving attention at Aldenham Works. Most important, of course, were the RCLs, whose overhauls were in full swing. A visit to the Works on 18th September 1980 sees two of them, RCL2241 and RCL2260 awaiting intake outside. The faded adverts, damage to its wings and missing radiator grille are testament to the latter's having been out of action in outside store for a long time.

Although the RCLs never changed bodies, their bodies were nevertheless separated from their running units when they were overhauled, both initially as Green Line coaches in 1971/72, and in 1980. RCL2220 illustrates this, and needed a lot of attention: it had been 'put out to grass' at Chelsham when its certificate of fitness expired in February 1978, and not used since! Such vehicles therefore took much longer to overhaul than the usual month or so in Aldenham Works!

Also separated from its running units that day, RCL2245 which had been used as a driver trainer after return to London Transport, still in Lincoln green livery, is undergoing overhaul and of note are the standard RM/RML-style wings with single headlamps, replacing its originals which had double ones. It has also had some new offside panels fitted.

Looking as good as new, RCL2237 awaits inspection and licensing after overhaul, repaint and varnishing in Aldenham's famous 'oven'. Of note is the fact that its wings are of the original RM-style with brake cooling grilles, now filled in, and therefore secondhand ones. This perfectly illustrates how various parts of buses under overhaul were freely interchanged.

Outside the Works also on 18th September 1980, RCL2244's overhaul is complete, and it awaits outshopping to Edmonton Garage, where it will enter service a couple of weeks later. A new Metrobus, destined to replace the ill-fated DMSs, stands in front of it.

On the same occasion, RMC1511 has just been repainted in red and also awaits despatch to its home garage from where it will resume training duties. It is interesting to compare the rear of this RMC with that of the RCL in the previous picture. The RMC has retained its platform doors, whereas those on the RCL have been removed, and two grabrails added to its platform area. Also, on the right of this view, green RMC1458 awaits repaint into red.

Another coach Routemaster awaiting attention in Aldenham that day, ex-British Airways KGJ613D, now numbered RMA38, is about to have its staircase removed and then be repainted red to take up duties as a training bus.

Sister vehicle RMA29 (KGJ603D) has had this special treatment, and waits to be licensed and sent out on to training duties. The metal structure on the right of the picture appears to be the staircase removed from one of these vehicles.

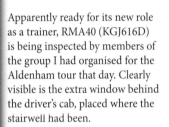

Apparently ready for its new role as a trainer, RMA40 (KGJ616D) is being inspected by members of the group I had organised for the Aldenham tour that day. Clearly visible is the extra window behind the driver's cab, placed where the stairwell had been.

By 25th March 1982, when I organised what would be my last tour of Aldenham Works, all regular staff buses there were RMAs. By now, they had received external in-house London Transport advertisements, and those on RMA16 are badly faded since it was usually stabled outside London Country's Two Waters (Hemel Hempstead) Garage where it was outstationed. It would be the last RMA staff bus in use, with B.E.L., in December 1987.

# THE RCLs' PREMATURE DEMISE

Regrettably, the RCL's had hardly been in service for a year when, thanks to the cheap fare policies of the Greater London Council which controlled London Transport, and whose Leader Ken Livingstone and Prime Minister Margaret Thatcher had a mutual loathing for each other, these policies were challenged in the High Court. This would lead to swingeing service cuts, and the premature withdrawal of the RCLs. However on 29th October 1981, they are still carrying on regardless: RCL2249 (SF) has a good load aboard at Manor House.

The winter of 1981/82 was a particularly snowy one, and would be the only one when the RCLs had to cope with such severe conditions as red buses. No doubt their crews and passengers, assuming they realised they had been, wished their doors had not been removed! On 12th December 1981, RCL2220 (EM) passes Lower Edmonton Station bound for Smithfield on the 279, and although the road itself has been cleared of snow, much of it remains on the pavements and grass verges.

By 29th May 1982, the Court ruling regarding cheap fares had gone against the G.L.C. and London Transport had a programme of service cuts devised. This affected the external advertisements on buses, and RCL2244 (EM) turning right at the Nag's Head, Holloway - where once an intricate web of trolleybus overhead wires almost blotted out the sun - has its front adverts extolling the cheap fares blanked out and a new one referring to the increases forced on L.T. put on the side. The RCLs were now even more indiscriminately used alongside RMs at both Edmonton and Stamford Hill; already it was being rumoured that they would soon be withdrawn as non-standard!

It is just a matter of time before the RCL's will be decreed non-standard on 29th July 1982, as RCL2260 (EM) passes Madras Place Cottages and Islington Central Library in Holloway Road, turning short at Highbury Corner on the 279. By now, this RCL - numerically the last one built - has been adopted as a showbus by staff at Edmonton Garage, and painted in pre-1965 L.T. red livery, with cream waistband and gold transfers. It has also regained its original twin-headlamps.

Although, as things turned out, the first programmed withdrawal of Routemasters involved Leyland-engined examples with obsolete electrical equipment, some 200 of which perished as a result of the 'Law Lords' cuts (on 4th September 1982), the non-standard RCLs were now in the firing line, too. On 22nd April 1983, RCL2246 (SF) has broken down when working the 253 near The Brecknock pub in Camden Road, Holloway and waits to be towed home. By coincidence, the very next day, another round of service cuts rendered more standard RMs surplus and in effect, one of these replaced this RCL which never ran again and was thus the first red one to be withdrawn.

Despite all the doom and gloom surrounding London Transport in the summer of 1983, its Golden Jubilee was celebrated with open days at a number of garages, including Edmonton whose RCL fleet was then still intact on 11th June 1983. The garage showbus, RCL2260 (EM), had pride of place amid the vehicle displays and has now received cream window surrounds in the same style as the RCLs had them in light green when they were new.

The continuing and ever escalating mutual antagonism between the G.L.C.'s Ken Livingstone and Prime Minister Margaret Thatcher led to the drafting of the Transport Bill, under which control of London Transport would be snatched from the Council by the Tory government. Their response to this was a poster campaign exhorting people to protest against it. On 7th January 1984, RCL2219 (EM) - now one of a dying breed - passes one of the posters in Hertford Road, Ponders End. Appropriately, it shows an RM, a type threatened by the change in legislation, too.

On Purim, 18th March 1984, RCL2222 (SF) has had a lively trip through Stamford Hill on the 253 amongst the rejoicing crowds, and accompanies stablemate M779 at Aldgate, Minories Bus Station where it would have been a regular when working Green Line route 721 between 1965 and 1971. Now, the sight of one of these splendid vehicles there would soon be a thing of the past, as their gradual withdrawal got into its stride.

Following on from its destruction of London Transport, which was split into two semi-autonomous companies, London Buses Ltd and London Underground Ltd, under the Tory government quango London Regional Transport at the end of June 1984, the Thatcher regime then set out to destroy the Greater London Council itself. In its last weeks of controlling London's buses, the Council had adverts posted on many of them protesting at this - alas, all to no avail. On 2nd June 1984, RCL2254 (EM) displays them when heading south along Tottenham High Road bus lane.

One of Stamford Hill's dwindling number of RCLs, RCL2251 (SF), changes crew at the westbound stop at Clapton Common on route 253 on 1st September 1984. Soon such sights here will be no more, and surely the sign advertising bus passes and travelcards at a nearby newsagents is a trip hazard?

Most ironically, withdrawn RCLs were stored at the former A.E.C. Works at Southall, where only four years previously many had been assembled after reacquisition prior to overhaul. On 28th September 1984, RCL2219 accompanies withdrawn RMs, DMSs and an MD in its former showroom.

Just over a week later, on 7th October 1984, a group of RCLs are parked in the yard outside the Works awaiting their fate, which however would be different to that of those of their fellows which had already reached the scrapyard.

On 17th November 1984, RCL2252(EM), one of the last red RCLs in service, has terminated at Liverpool Street Station on route 149 - the route for which forty of them had been overhauled only just over four years previously.

# SIGHTSEEING

After languishing in store for a year or more, twelve of the RCL's were again reprieved and given a new lease of life, this time replacing O.P.O. vehicles on London Transport's Round London Sightseeing Tour. Therefore history repeated itself! Along with a number of RMs', they were refurbished and repainted at Aldenham, but various work on them was done at garages. On 22nd March 1986, RCL2248 is given a steam clean to its engine in Loughton Garage, which had excellent maintenance facilities and, ironically, never operated RM-types. Several were dealt with there at this period, and sadly the garage closed two months later.

Battersea Garage, which had closed in November 1985, was reopened to house the sightseeing buses: RCL2243 and RCL2260 have just arrived there on 28th March 1986. The latter again has single-headlamp wings, this time from an early RM.

One of the first public appearances made by the sightseeing RCLs was that of RCL2220 at the Barking Bus Rally, of which I was the main organiser, on 6th April 1986. It is still on trade plates and bears advertising for what is now dubbed 'The Original London Transport Sightseeing Tour' in an effort to upstage various 'cowboy' operators on competing ventures. As may be seen, it is in pre-1965 L.T. livery too. Its rather odd blinds reflect the fact that a coach service between London and Birmingham was operated by the L.R.T. subsidiary London Coaches from Battersea Garage at this time, but it is very unlikely that RCLs ever operated it!

By 8th May 1986, the surviving RCLs were in use on the O.L.T.S.T. as it became to be known. This rear view of RCL2243 at Tower Hill shows that they originally retained the rear platform arrangement they had had when in use as buses, without doors.

Later the same day, the heavens have opened as RCL2260 hopefully awaits trade on the O.L.T.S.T's dedicated stand in Victoria Street outside the Circle and District Line station. These vehicles, and even the standard RMs used on the tour, must have been a welcome change from the shuddering DMSs and Metrobuses used on it previously.

Further coach Routemasters were added to the sightseeing fleet in the autumn of 1986 in the shape of six RMAs previously used as staff buses. On 9th November that year, RMA25 has just arrived at Battersea and stands in the garage yard next to RCL2241. As may be observed, this has been re-fitted with platform doors, as all of its fellows there were. They differed from those the RCLs had when new.

On a cold, crisp 31st January 1987, no doubt the platform doors on RCL2241 are a benefit to its passengers on the O.L.T.S.T. as it circumnavigates Parliament Square. Otherwise smart, it shows signs of damage to its radiator grille and bonnet.

In addition to sightseeing tour duties, the RCLs and RMAs were available for private hires, too. On 18th March 1987, RCL2245 has taken guests to a wedding at the church of St. Julius the Martyr in Acton, but for some reason does not carry the customary white ribbons!

In the yard at Battersea on 25th April 1967, RMA15 and RMA22, both of which had seen previous use as staff buses, are two more additions to the sightseeing fleet. As with RCL2220 shown earlier, they display blinds for London Coaches' services.

94

To mark the demise of Green Line route 706 on the evening 29th May 1987, two RCLs (2241 and 2250) returned to their former haunts on the original routes 704 and 705 to work it specially: RCL2250 turns from Buckingham Palace Road onto Elizabeth Bridge, Victoria.

Less appropriate on this occasion was the use of former Airways coach and staff bus RMA26, which of course had never worked on Green Line services in real life! It awaits the off in Buckingham Palace Road. And the spelling 'Seven Oaks' for one of the via points on both vehicles' blinds is odd to say the least!

In the more usual role of a sightseeing tour bus, RMA15 collects tourists on the O.L.T.S.T.'s dedicated stand on the forecourt of Baker Street Station on 16th April 1989. Operations had been moved from Battersea to Wandsworth Garage following the latter's closure for normal service buses in July 1987.

Another change to befall the RCLs was the conversion of all the survivors on the sightseeing tour, with the exception of RCL2260, to convertible open-toppers. RCL2245 passes St. Paul's Cathedral in this guise in August 1991. Also the gold L.T. fleetname has been replaced by branding for the tour.

In February 1992, the same RCL (2245) passes Mansion House Station on the sightseeing tour with the detachable centre section of its roof in place. Interestingly, this matches the pattern of the original, complete with the short amidships bay.

In line with London Regional Transport policy, the sightseeing operations were privatised in May 1992 as 'London Coaches', which now operated 'The Original London Sightseeing Tour'. Along with this, some of their Routemasters were adorned in garish all-over advertising liveries. On 20th April 1993, RCL2245 is sullied with this dreadful advert for junk food as it approaches the junction of Buckingham Gate and Victoria Street.

For the first few years, Routemasters of all three types (RM, RCL, RMA) were retained by London Coaches and given a new standard livery. In October 1993, RCL2250 appears to have only two passengers aboard as it heads south along King William Street, sporting the new entity's livery.

In February 1994, RMA15 also carries the revised O.L.S.T. livery when passing Horse Guards Parade. Whether it is actually working a private charter, or the sightseeing tour itself, is unclear. Not long after this picture was taken, these were withdrawn from sightseeing work.

# DOCKLANDS EXPRESS

Whilst RCLs and RMAs were returned to use as sightseeing buses in 1986 and 1987, RMCs continued to be used in dwindling numbers as trainers, though their numbers dropped dramatically after the closure of the Chiswick Training School. But that was not the end for the class. A surprise early in 1989 was the refurbishment of six former trainer RMCs for use on a new 'Beckton Express' route X15. This was originally a 'with the flow' rush hour service that ran from Beckton to Trafalgar Square in the morning rush hour, and then from Oxford Circus to Beckton in the evening. In the off-peak period, buses ran on the traditional route 15 with which the X15 effectively inter-worked from Upton Park Garage. On the first day of this arrangement, Monday 6th March 1989, RMC1461 (U) heads around the one-way system behind Aldgate Station for East Ham after the morning rush hour. Of note is the special livery, with gold window surrounds, and the fact that the RMC has received a standard RM/RML-style front blind box. The effect is somewhat spoilt by it having odd wings - the nearside being an original RMC one, the offside being from an RCL or perhaps an RMA!

Also on the first day of this operation, RMC1490 (U) turns from Mincing Walk into Great Tower Street, having been diverted owing to roadworks in Eastcheap. Of note here is that these RMCs have retained their platform doors, above which the X15 blind is still shown in error when the bus is working route 15. This one too has odd wings, but with an RMC one on the offside and an RCL/RMA one on the nearside.

This rear view of RMC1496 (U) passing Monument Station on the 15 that first day illustrates the rear-end treatment of these vehicles in the special Beckton Express livery. Here, the conductor has forgotten to change the rear destination blind, as it is really heading for East Ham.

*Above:* The RMCs retained their original coach seating, and RMC1458 has given me a comfortable ride from Monument to Ludgate Hill, where it is among a queue of Routemasters waiting to cross Ludgate Circus. The building works on the left are for the new tunnel taking Thameslink trains beneath Holborn Viaduct Station into the new St. Paul's Thameslink Station.

*Right:* Dusk falls as RMC1458 (U) crosses Ludgate Circus heading in the other direction on one of the X15's evening journeys to 'East Beckton, Cyprus'. This terminus was once referred to as 'Royal Albert Dock' when buses on routes 101 and 147 terminated there.

On 22nd September 1989, RMC1496 (U) contrasts with the run-down and still blitz-scarred scenery at Custom House Station - the regeneration of Docklands has yet to reach this area! The route had been introduced between the peaks during the week, and on Saturday shopping hours, in June of that year.

For some reason, a seventh RMC, RMC1485 (U) was refurbished for the X15 a few weeks after its introduction. In May 1990, however, it is giving rides at a special event at Epping Station commemorating the 125th anniversary of the railway's opening there.

The Beckton Express RMCs inevitably found their way onto normal bus routes 15 and 15B irrespective of interworking with the X15. In July 1991, RMC1496 (U) crosses Ludgate Circus on the latter, which had special yellow destination blinds to emphasise that this route ran via Bank rather than via the Tower. Also of note here is that the railway bridge across the foot of Ludgate Hill has been removed, and Holborn Viaduct Station closed following the opening of St. Paul's Thameslink Station.

Although route X15 was converted to O.P.O. in November 1991, some of the RMCs remained at Upton Park Garage, being used alongside RMLs and a few RMs on routes 15 and 15B. In May 1992, RMC1513 (U) - another with odd wings and another of those originally refurbished for the X15 - calls at Charing Cross Station on its way to Ladbroke Grove, two months before the 15 was withdrawn west of Paddington.

The sixth original 'Beckton Express' RMC, RMC1456 (U), heads west at St. Paul's Churchyard on 17th July 1992, the last day route 15 ventured beyond Paddington. It too has odd wings!

In addition to the RMCs used at Upton Park Garage, two RMAs were refurbished for service there. One, RMA8 had latterly been a B.E.L. staff bus, and on 12th September 1992 is in use specially on route 111 in conjunction with an open day at Hounslow Garage. Here, it passes the garage overtaking a Metrobus usually employed on the route.

During their time in east London, the former Beckton Express RMCs were firm favourites at bus rallies and special events. On 5th September 1993, RMC1458 and RMC1513, both now transferred to Bow Garage, are providing a special service over part of the old Green Line route 718 for the Chingford, Royal Forest Hotel event, of which I was one of the organisers. They are outside this former terminus, which had closed 25 years previously at the onset of LT's Reshaping Plan.

Later in September 1993, RMC1458 (BW) crosses Oxford Circus bound for route 8's new western terminus of Victoria Station, to where it was diverted following the 25's old routeing from Bond Street in July 1992.

Bow's second RMC, RMC1513 (BW) has just negotiated the one-way system at St. Paul's Cathedral in October 1993. No one seemed to mind that these former coaches seated fifteen fewer passengers than the RMLs normally working routes 8 and 15, perhaps because they were more comfortable and still had their platform doors to keep the cold out in winter.

*Above:* A very full RMC1485 (BW) picks up and sets down passengers at Enfield Chase Station on 26th February 1994 working special route 304 from Oakwood to Chingford. It has recently been transferred to Bow Garage, repainted, and given gold London Transport fleetnames. Bow's Operations Manager Jon Batchelor is at the wheel.

*Right:* The other RMA at Upton Park was RMA5, which quite bizarrely had hitherto been a trainer, so had to have its staircase reinstated! It is beginning to look a little shabby when working route 15 through Oxford Circus in March 1994. I well remember intending passengers in Oxford Street being confused by these RMAs, looking in vain for a rear entrance!

Bow's third RMC, RMC1485 (BW) also saw use on route 8, on which it carries a standing load heading west at Tottenham Court Road Station in May 1994, shortly before privatisation saw Bow and Upton Park Garages, and consequently their former coach Routemasters, privatised to become part of the Stagecoach 'empire'.

# ODDITIES

Inevitably, there were oddities amongst the coach Routemasters. For some months after their withdrawal from service on route 175 at Romford, North Street Garage, RMA6 was kept there as an engineers' bus, attending to breakdowns and even towing them, as of course it still had a towing facility from when it had had a trailer on the Airport Express service. It ran on trade plates and in its front nearside lower deck window it had a slipboard saying 'LTE.North St. Engineers". These are visible in this view of it outside the garage on 5th February 1977. Subsequently, it was used as a staff bus.

This rear view of RCL2232, the only one of the class to be painted red when on training duties for London Transport, shows quite clearly that it still has its original platform doors. These were removed on overhaul when all of them were painted red for route 149, and the dozen used as sightseeing buses were later fitted with a different style of doors. It passes Fullwell Cross, Barkingside on 18th March 1979.

An oddity appearance-wise was RMC1502, which carried the body originally on RMC1469 which had been rebuilt with a wider front blindbox as a pilot for the RCLs. It retained this for the rest of its life; this view finds it after return to London Transport on training duties at the Archway Station stand in MacDonald Road on 16th October 1979.

London Transport bought back 41 of the 43 RCLs, forty of which were eventually overhauled as red buses for use on route 149. The other one, RCL2221, was fitted out as a mobile exhibition and cinema and painted in dark green and yellow Shillibeer livery to commemorate the 150th anniversary of London's buses in 1979. In this guise it attended many special events, and was still doing so on 7th June 1980, when it heads for home at Chiswick Works along Bromley Road after an open day at Catford Garage.

Prototype Routemaster coach RMC4 was retained by London Country after their other RM-types had been withdrawn, and used as a special events vehicle. On 13th July 1980, it is manoeuvred into place at an open day at their Crawley, Tinsley Green overhaul works commemorating the 80th anniversary of Green Line coaches. By now, it has been rebuilt with opening front upper-deck windows.

*Above*: Though not in itself unusual, RMC1487 was a strange case historically. Repurchased from London Country along with all but two of the standard RMCs, it was repainted in red and prepared for use as a trainer. It stands in Stonebridge Park Garage in this condition on 16th May 1981. However, in the event it was never used as a trainer and instead sold privately, apparently to a friend of a senior L.T. official who 'pulled strings'. It later passed into preservation and, during the mid-1980s, I was briefly a co-owner of it. But where is it now?

*Left*: By 27th June 1981 when it is taking part in an open day at Finchley Garage, RCL2221 has been repainted into a new livery of red with a yellow waistband and window surrounds and is still in use as a cinema and exhibition vehicle.

During the summer of 1981, RCL2256 (SF) was involved in a serious rear-end collision, which demolished its back. It was therefore rebuilt with a standard RM/RML rear end, and at first sight looks indistinguishable from one of that type when passing through Camden Town on the 253 on 26th August 1981. What gives it away however is the smaller used ticket box on the platform bulkhead. It also lacked the offside lower-deck emergency window exit fitted to RMLs. This vehicle would probably have been withdrawn if the accident had happened a few months later when the 'Law Lords' cuts would enforce Routemaster withdrawals. Indeed, RCL2233 was withdrawn early as a result of a rear-end collision soon after they commenced.

RMC1515 was deroofed when working as a trainer from Upton Park Garage, but instead of being scrapped, was converted to an open-topper for use on private hire work. However, when not in such use, it continued in its training role, as here at Wood Green Station on 12th April 1988.

Trainer RMC1510 suffered a similar accident, and was likewise converted to an open-topper. By now with London Buses' subsidiary CentreWest, it ran specially on route 140 in conjunction with an open day at Harrow Weald Garage on 7th April 1990 and this view finds it heading through Northolt on the way to Heathrow.

CentreWest also retained trainer RMC1492 as a recruitment and training vehicle. It was based at Alperton Garage, where it stands on show during an open-day there on 30th May 1992. Its blind tells how it is fifty years old, well not quite at this date - but who cares!

Also in May 1992, open-top RMC1510 (X) was used in normal service on route 15, and in this view, runs out from Westbourne Park Garage bound for Aldwych. When 'new' route 23 replaced the western section of the 15 two months later, it worked that route too.

RMA57 (NMY654E) was bought by London Transport amongst the last batch of the class, and though in serviceable condition never used by them. It was sold to a preservationist in 1982, and restored to 1969 B.E.A. orange and white livery. Three years later, it was sold again to members of the ill-fated Docklands Road Transport Museum, one of whom was myself. On 20th September 1986, it is providing a free service between our Transport Bazaar at East Ham Town Hall, behind which it is parked, and the North Woolwich Station railway museum - the latter too is now defunct! The RMA, however, lives on today with a south London private operator who specialises in private hire work.

An oddity amongst the RMAs that were bought by London Transport but never used was RMA49. Rather than going for scrap, it was acquired by Blue Triangle, and on New Year's Day 1989, specially works Essex County Council route 504 between Bishops Stortford and Walthamstow, parts of which had replaced Green Line route 702 some years before. Here, it calls at The Spotted Dog pub in the village of Fivechimneys near Epping, where I was enjoying a few pints at the time.

RCL2239 was also acquired by Blue Triangle, after its premature withdrawal from route 149, and it too worked route 504 on New Year's Day 1989. Here, it calls at The Carpenters Arms in Thornwood Common, with my old mate Jim Owen at the wheel. I was also enjoying a pint there at the time.

Another RMA to see service with an independent operator in the London area was RMA14 (KGJ602D), one of a number bought by Green Rover of Watford, and used mainly on school contracts. On 22nd January 1990, however, this one is specially working route 310A between Hertford and Waltham Cross in conjunction with the Hoddesdon Model Railway Exhbition. It calls opposite the civic centre in Hoddesdon where this was staged in this view. This one had previously been used as a staff bus.

Coach Routemasters turned up in London after sale by London Transport on rail replacement services, too. On 7th September 1992, RMA52, which is now in the fleet of Time Travel and usually used for private hires, calls at Angel Station on a replacement service for the Northern Line while that station's antiquated island platform is being removed and the station substantially rebuilt. It too had been a staff bus.

*Above:* Although about half of the RCL class, and a few RMCs and RMAs were scrapped in the early 1980s, a good few survived to see service in Central London after the privatisation of London Buses in the mid-1990s for much longer than anyone could have foreseen at that time. Although sold by London Buses, RMA49 still saw use for a while working on Blue Triangle's 'Official London Sightseeing Tour', though not many sightseers are aboard as it passes Trafalgar Square in November 1994.

*Right:* The RMCs at Bow and Upton Park Garages continued running on routes 8 and 15 after privatisation, though an irritating fad was registering some of them: this has happened to RMC1456 (U), beneath the Christmas lights at Oxford Circus in December 1994..

One surprise at this juncture was the repainting of East London's RMC1461 in original 1962 Green Line livery in 1994, to coincide with the 40th anniversary of the appearance of RM1. Latterly a Beckton Express vehicle, it ran in normal service on route 15, but also made appearances at special events, as on 25th February 1995 when passing Enfield Town Station on route 304.

RMC1464 was another former trainer RMC to be converted to open-top, for use as a private hire vehicle by Leaside Buses. However on a cold, crisp 2nd November 1995, it has most unusually been put in normal service on route 73, though few passengers appear to have braved the cold to see the sights in Stoke Newington and Stamford Hill from its upper deck as it approaches South Tottenham Station!

Other RMCs were sold off following their retirement as trainers for London Buses. Some went to preservationists, but others were acquired by small independent operators. An example of the latter is RMC1462, bought by Nostalgiabus for private hire duties. On a murky December 1995 day, is passes Grosvenor Gardens, Victoria working a Circle and District Line replacement service between Embankment and South Kensington.

The two Upton Park RMAs were also kept on for a few years by Stagecoach East London working route 15. They also proved ideal for the special limited stop 718 service to and from the North Weald Bus Rally: on 29th June 1997, RMA5 (U) lays over at the Airfield. Both were converted to left-hand drive the following year and exported to Portugal to work for Stagecoach there.

By 3rd August 2001, RMC1485 (U) has been transferred from Bow to Upton Park Garage and also repainted in Stagecoach East London's standard livery. It overtakes one of the then newly-introduced low-floor double-deckers at Aldwych on route 15.

By April 2002, Leaside Buses had long since metamorphosed into Arriva London, but the name 'Leaside Travel' was retained for their private hire business. So was open-top RMC1464, which is promoting the operator in Enfield Town. Of note is the reinstatement of the offside number blind box, in which Leaside's 'swan' symbol - a relic of the old L.T. Leaside District - is displayed.

Numerically the first production RMC, RMC1453 was also retained for private hire work by Leaside. On 8th June 2002, it has officiated at a wedding at St. Martin's-In-The-Fields at Trafalgar Square. Shame about its battered front dome, though!

RMC1485 (U) survived until the last day of crew operation on route 15, and was latterly reregistered with what at first appears to be a Scottish registration. On 9th August 2003, it heads east along Regent Street. Curiously, on the final day three weeks later, it was 485CLT again!

Green RMC1461 (U) also lasted until the end on route 15. On that last day, 29th August 2003, I caught this view from the window of The Liberty Bounds pub on Tower Hill of its final journey into town as dusk was falling.

Another coach Routemaster restored to original Green Line livery to see passenger service in London was RCL2260. Now with Blue Triangle, it was one of many ex-London Transport buses to be used on rail replacement service following a derailment which damaged the important junction at Camden Town on the Northern Line, causing both branches through central London to be closed for several weeks. On 27th October 2003, it sets off from East Finchley.

# SPECIAL WORKINGS

Coach Routemasters often ran specially on the last days of Routemaster operation in their final years. One of the former Beckton Express RMCs, RMC1513, ended up with Metroline as a private hire vehicle. On 26th March 2004, it ran in service on the last day of crew operation on route 98 from Willesden Garage, from where it has just set off emitting a cloud of exhaust in Willesden High Road.

After terminating at Oxford Circus, RMC1513 returned to Willesden on route 6, whose last day of crew operation it also was. It escorts an RT doing the same approaching Warwick Avenue Station.

The special workings on routes 6 and 98's last day of operation were outdone by even more on the last day of Routemasters on route 8 on 4th June 2004. Stagecoach's own RMC1456 and RMC1461 worked, along with privately owned RMC1469, which had been restored to original livery, and rebuilt with the RCL-style blindbox this stocknumber had before first overhaul. It has just set me down in High Holborn for a drink in the Penderels Oak that last evening.

Four weeks later, on 2nd July 2004, it is route 7's last day of Routemaster operation. The former CentreWest open-top RMC1510 (X) has been inherited by First London, and is specially working the route in Westbourne Grove.

Route 390 was the last Routemaster-operated route in London to be introduced, on 1st February 2003. It converted to O.P.O. after only nineteen months, and on their last day of operation, 3rd September 2004, Metroline's RMC1513 works it specially in Bloomsbury Street.

Complete with its detachable top, RCL2220 works specially on route 12's last day of Routemaster operation on 5th November 2004 as it rounds Addington Street roundabout at the southern end of Waterloo Bridge. It is in the Ensignbus heritage fleet at this time.

Recently refurbished for the Ensignbus heritage fleet, RMA58 was one of many guest buses used on route 19's final day of crew operation on 1st April 2005. It heads north along Upper Street, Islington in this view.

Former Beckton Express RMC1456, still with its silly registration, specially worked route 38 on its final day of Routemaster operation, 28th October 2005. Here, it turns from Graham Road into Mare Street, Hackney. It is one of a number of special workings that continued beyond the 38's current terminus at Clapton Pond to its former haunts in the East, in this case Leyton Green.

Arriva's RMC1453 was one of many guest vehicles used on route 159 - the last London fully Routemaster-operated route of all. On its last full day of crew operation, Friday 8th December, the weather was absolutely foul, this view of it at Kennington Church shows.

Even the withdrawal of normal Routemaster operation in London in 2005 was not the end of coach Routemasters running here in service. In June 2010, Arriva's open-top RMC1464 was one of two amongst other special vehicles working on route 123 to commemorate its 50th annivesary. It approaches the junction of Lordship Lane and the Roundway in Tottenham here.

RMC1453 was the other one used on the 123 that day. It calls at Gants Hill Station running in to Tottenham Garage (which operated the 123 at the time) here. When it was new (numerically!) in 1962, it would have passed that point on Green Line route 715A.

Other special appearances of coach Routemasters in normal service in London have been made in more recent times to commemorate the centenary of long-established bus routes. On 17th June 2012, open-top RMC1464 is one of several vehicles doing so on route 38. It contrasts with modern O.P.O. buses at Islington, Angel.

Even in the present decade, more than fifty years after they were built, coach Routemasters may still be seen at London's service other than commemorative duty! In April 2014, Metroline's RMC1513 heads north in a gridlocked New Oxford Street on the day of an all-out tube strike, trying to reach Islington, Angel as an extra on route 38.

Shortly after being rebuilt with a replica of its original front end, the first coach Routemaster of all, RMC4, is in The London Bus Company's heritage fleet when working part of the original Green Line route 718 to the North Weald Bus Rally, where it arrives on 21st June 2015. As things turned out, this was the last bus rally there after almost 35 years and I had been one of the main organisers at it between 1985 and 2012.

# THE RMFs

In the early 1960s, many operators opted for forward-entrance double-deckers, therefore London Transport decided to try the concept. In the summer of 1962, RMF1254 was built: this was basically an RML with a forward entrance, seating 69 passengers as opposed to 72 on an RML. It was exhibited at the 1962 Commercial Motor Show dressed up for route 104, but the busmen's unions refused to operate it. So instead it was sent to various operators as a demonstrator for the type, and then used by B.E.A. (who already had a similarly-configured A.E.C. Regent V) on their Earl's Court to Heathrow Express service. This led to B.E.A. buying 65 similar Routemasters, but of the shorter length and with coach seating as illustrated earlier in this book. It stands at Heathrow Airport on 24th September 1966, shortly before the new coaches arrived.

The only other operator to buy Routemasters was Northern General, who operated them in the Tyne and Wear area. Fifty of them were delivered in 1964/65, and they differed from the prototype by having Leyland engines, sliding windows and also non-opening front upper-deck windows. The original RMF was also sold to them after its stint with B.E.A. When their withdrawal began in the late 1970s, some came to the London area. One of these, FPT589C (Northern General No. 2119, later 3103) was acquired by Obsolete Fleet, painted in London Transport livery and given the stocknumber RMF2791. It is being fuelled at a filling station in Victoria prior to taking up service on the RLST on 10th July 1978.

Smartly painted in standard London Transport livery, Obsolete Fleet's EUP407B, originally Northern General's 2107 and later 3091, has been dubbed 'RMF2762' when passing Trafalgar Square on the Round London Sightseeing Tour on 15th April 1979. Another non-standard feature on these vehicles was the fixed front windscreen, which however was also used on the RMA's. On the other hand, these vehicles have acquired standard RM/RML style front blindboxes.

Such was London Transport's despair about the shortcomings of the DMSs in 1979/80, that they were determined to lay their hands on any Routemasters they could get to replace them. Having acquired most of the former London Country Routemasters, and all of the British Airways Coaches when they were retired, they then proceeded to snap up the last surviving Northern General examples, which were given fleet numbers RMF2761 onwards - in some cases duplicating those given those on the RLST! At Aldenham on 18th September 1980, RCN696 (former Northern General No. 2096, later 3080, and allocated stocknumber RMF2769) is one of two that had been sent there for inspection prior to a possible overhaul. It was hoped to operate them on routes 26, ironically at Finchley who had refused the prototype in 1962, and 45. However inspection of the vehicles apparently found a number of non-standard features which meant they were not deemed worth overhauling. Sadly, most of those which had reached London Transport went for scrap. Others, however, found use as sightseeing buses, or were preserved and are still around today.

Fortunately, prototype RMF1254, which had become No.3129 in the Northern General fleet, was secured by a preservationist and so avoided the sad fate of most of those that came to London Transport. On 17th June 1981, it works an enthusiasts' tour for the North London Transport Society in Lordship Lane, Wood Green where it provides an interesting contrast with a standard RML. Of note is the fact that its side windows have been altered to Northern General's standard sliding type, though the originals remain at the front. It also has a one-piece windscreen and a standard Northern General front blind display in place of its original L.T. one.

An oddity was former Northern General No.2106 (later 3090) which was converted to open-top by Obsolete Fleet, and used as a sightseeing bus. On 29th August 1983, it works the Tour of Back Street London at Camden Lock.

Of those Northern General RMFs which were either not used on London Sightseeing work, or bought but not used by London Transport, their No. 2095 (RCN695) was one of the first to pass into preservation, and initially smartly restored to N.B.C. corporate red N.G.T. livery. It ran in service on route 339 connecting Epping Station with North Weald Airfield for the bus rally there on 23rd June 1985. Here, it turns from Epping High Street into Station Road on its way to collect another load of spectators for the rally.

By October 1985, EUP406B has actually been acquired by London Transport for use on the RLST, being given the stock number RMT2793. This picture finds it crossing Waterloo Bridge.

Blue Triangle chipped in to the London Sightseeing trade with a Northern General RMF too - FPT588C (ex-N.G.T. 2118 and then 3102) has been converted to open-top and dubbed 'RMO2118' when heading past St. Paul's Cathedral on 29th May 1987.

Blue Triangle's RMF FPT588C later passed to The Big Bus Company, who also operated London Sightseeing tours. Here, it passes Marble Arch in March 1993. Of note is the fact that its blindbox has been panelled over, RMA-style.

RMF1254 was fully restored to original 1962 London Transport condition in time for the 'RM50' celebrations at Finsbury Park in the summer of 2004. It finally saw normal service in London on 28th October 2005, working as a guest vehicle on route 38's last day of crew operation. That morning, it picks up passengers in Essex Road, Islington. The young lady at the rear of the bus is puzzled that she cannot find an entrance at the rear! Passengers were similarly confused when a couple of RMAs were used on route 15 in the early 1990s, as mentioned earlier in this book.

# WHAT MIGHT HAVE BEEN - THE FRM

In the mid-1960s, work was put in hand to design Routemasters with front entrances and rear engines, in line with current practice exemplified by the Leyland Atlantean and Daimler Fleetline. It seems four prototypes were envisaged, but in the event only one was actually completed and perhaps this explains why it was registered KGY4D rather than KGY1D. What happened to the other three can only be surmised, as a government diktat by Harold Wilson's transport minister Barbara Castle decreed that, henceforth, London Transport must buy 'off-the-peg' buses like everyone else, and not their own purpose-built designs. On 28th April 1967, what was christened FRM1 makes what is possibly its first public appearance in Vauxhall Bridge Road, Victoria. It was said to have been constructed from 60% standard Routemaster parts, though its non-opening windows (with forced air ventilation) seem to belie that somewhat. An odd feature is the full-depth emergency door on the offside behind the staircase; RML's merely had an outward-opening offside lower-deck window as an emergency exit.

FRM1 (AR) entered service in July 1967 on route 76, alongside the similarly-configured XAs, but suffered an engine fire a few months later. When it was repaired, it was fitted with opening windows which made it look more like a normal Routemaster! The ventilating slat above the front windows, as also fitted originally to early RMs 5-354, was retained. Shortly after this modification, it passes the roundabout at the southern end of Waterloo Bridge on 16th December 1967. The bus was also used on rush-hour route 34B when at Tottenham.

*Right:* When route 76's XAs had been transferred to South Croydon Garage, the FRM went with them, initially working the one-bus route 233, linking West Croydon with the new Roundshaw Estate, built on the site of the old Croydon Aerodrome. The estate is still under construction as it loads up there on 23rd March 1971. The vehicle has now been given the 'unfilled roundel' livery used on new DMS deliveries at this period.

*Below:* The FRM was also used on routes 234 (weekday) and 234B (Saturday & Sunday) when based at South Croydon. It stands at Selsdon, Farley Road terminus on 14th July 1972 on the latter, which was a far cry from its original haunts on the busy 76.

The FRM had its first overhaul in the autumn of 1973, and was sent to Potters Bar Garage to work the one-bus route 284, which was a circular service liking the High Street with the railway station, replacing an MBS. On 18th October that year, it heads south along the Great North Road north of the town. It carries the new solid-roundel livery later adopted for new and overhauled London Transport buses. Of note is the new ventilator below the windscreen where an LT bullseye had originally been located.

A second overhaul followed late in 1977, after which FRM1 went to Stockwell Garage to work the Round London Sightseeing Tour on which it passes the Bank of England on 16th February 1978. If London Transport had been permitted to develop this type, it is possible that they may have carried on where the RMLs left off, and since they would have been capable of one-man operation, maybe the nightmare of the 1970s that London Transport suffered thanks to the MB, SM and DM types would never have happened...but it was not to be!

On 3rd September 2004, the unique FRM1 - now long exiled to the L.T. Museum - returned to its original garage, Tottenham, to take part in the funeral rites for Routemasters on route 73. That afternoon, it heads south along Pentonville Road from Islington, Angel, but is only venturing as far as Euston rather than battling its way to Victoria through evening rush hour traffic in the West End.

FRM1 is still in the care of the London Transport Museum today, occasionally being used at special events. On 19th July 2013, it has returned to its original route, the 76, to celebrate its centenary, when heading along Hertford Road, Dalston.

# STRETCHING POINTS - THE ERMs

Although they were not, strictly speaking, 'coach Routemasters', I am including the final variation of the Routemaster class, the ERM, that London Buses operated, since they do not really fit in to the other two volumes in this series, on the RM and the RML. These were RMs operating the Original London Transport Sightseeing Tour that had already been converted to open-top in 1986. For the 1990 season, some of these were literally cut in half amidships and fitted with an extra full-length bay, taken from scrap RMs, to provide eight extra seats on each deck! This gave them 80 seats, and made them longer than RMLs and RCLs, in whose style the two sub-frames were connected beneath their elongated bodies. In July 1990, ERM84 heads down Duke Street Hill alongside London Bridge Station. 'ERM' denoted 'extended RM', just as 'ER' had done in the original classification of the RMLs.

Sporting the OLST's new livery but prior to privatisation, ERM235 climbs Ludgate Hill in August 1991. By now, a 'hop on, hop off' facility had been adopted for the tour, dubbed 'London Plus' to compete with other Sightseeing operators doing likewise.

For some reason, ERM90 still retains the original OLST livery in May 1992, after its operation had been privatised as 'London Coaches'. It has just entered the eastern end of Victoria Embankment from the Blackfriars Bridge underpass.

Just up the hill outside the Law Courts in The Strand on the same day, this rear view of ERM242 emphasises its length as it heads east towards Fleet Street and St. Paul's.

In common with London Coaches' RCLs and RMAs towards the end of their use on London sightseeing work, the ERMs were subjected to all-over advertising. ERM235 heads west along Victoria Embankment in December 1995, when few or its passengers are hardy enough to brave sitting upstairs!

# END OF THE ROAD

On 5th October 1981, three of the RMFs which had been acquired from Northern General by London Transport make a sad sight in C.F. Booth's Rotherham scrapyard. The two closest to the camera had been at Aldenham a year previously, as illustrated above.

As mentioned earlier, the 'Law Lords' service cuts caused the premature withdrawal of the RCLs, and by 30th August 1984, many had been withdrawn and sent to the Yorkshire scrapyards. RCL2224 makes a sad sight at the yard of Wigley's of Carlton.

At the same yard, RCL2236 also awaits its fate along with RM251 and RM1678.

These two views show all that is left of RCL2234 after Wigley's scrapmen have dealt with it. A mass of seat frames form a backdrop to the second view, in which the strengthening bars amidships which supported the RCLs' and RMLs' extra short bay may also be discerned. Fortunately, about half of the RCL class and many RMAs and RMCs, along with the lone FRM and a few RMFs, survived the Thatcher years and many are still around in 2018! Indeed, one RMA has been lengthened by the insertion of an extra full bay, ERM-style, whilst an ERM has also been fitted with a roof again. But these vehicles run outside the London area, so have no place in this book.